JAMES FRITZ

James Fritz is a playwright from South London.

Plays for stage include *The Flea* (The Yard Theatre); *Cashmoney Now* (The Big House); *Lava* (Fifth Word/Soho Theatre); *The Fall* (National Youth Theatre/Southwark Playhouse); *Parliament Square* (Royal Exchange/Bush Theatre); *Start Swimming* (Young Vic); *Ross & Rachel* (Assembly/BAC/59E59); *Four Minutes Twelve Seconds* (Hampstead Theatre/Trafalgar Studios) and *Lines* (Rosemary Branch Theatre).

Plays for audio include *The Test Batsman's Room at the End of the World*, *Dear Harry Kane*, *Eight Point Nine Nine*, *Death of a Cosmonaut*, *Comment Is Free* (all BBC Radio 4) and *Skyscraper Lullaby* (Audible Originals).

He has won the Critics' Circle Theatre Award for Most Promising Playwright, a Bruntwood Prize for Playwriting, the Imison and Tinniswood BBC Audio Drama Awards and the ARIA Radio Academy Award for Best Drama on two separate occasions. He has also been nominated for the Olivier Award for Outstanding Achievement in an Affiliate Theatre and was runner-up in the 2013 Verity Bargate Award.

**Other Playwright Collections
from Nick Hern Books**

Mike Bartlett

Jez Butterworth

Alexi Kaye Campbell

Caryl Churchill

Ayub Khan Din

David Edgar

Kevin Elyot

Ella Hickson

Robert Holman

Stephen Jeffreys

Deirdre Kinahan

Lucy Kirkwood

Liz Lochhead

Kenneth Lonergan

Conor McPherson

Mark O'Rowe

Evan Placey

Jack Thorne

debbie tucker green

Enda Walsh

Steve Waters

Nicholas Wright

JAMES FRITZ

Plays: One

Four Minutes Twelve Seconds
Ross & Rachel
twins
Parliament Square
Lava
Skyscraper Lullaby

with an Introduction by the author

NICK HERN BOOKS

London

www.nickhernbooks.co.uk

A Nick Hern Book

James Fritz Plays: One first published in Great Britain as a paperback original in 2023 by Nick Hern Books Limited, The Glasshouse, 49a Goldhawk Road, London W12 8QP

This collection copyright © 2023 James Fritz
Introduction copyright © 2023 James Fritz

Four Minutes Twelve Seconds copyright © 2014, 2023
Ross & Rachel copyright © 2015, 2023
twins copyright © 2023
Parliament Square copyright © 2017, 2023
Lava copyright © 2018, 2023
Skyscraper Lullaby copyright © 2023

James Fritz has asserted his right to be identified as the author of these works

Four Minutes Twelve Seconds was first published by Methuen Drama, an imprint of Bloomsbury Publishing Plc, and is reproduced with permission.

Cover image: *The Dog* by Francisco José de Goya y Lucientes; Prado, Madrid, Spain/Bridgeman Images

Designed and typeset by Nick Hern Books, London
Printed in Great Britain by Mimeo Ltd, Huntingdon, Cambridgeshire PE29 6XX

ISBN   978 1 83904 284 3

www.nickhernbooks.co.uk/environmental-policy

Contents

An Interview with James Fritz
September 2023

Hi James. Thanks for sitting down with me.

Thank you! This is really exciting.

So sorry I was late. This is a nice place.

Yeah, I love this café, it's close to the library where I sometimes work.

So I don't know how much they've told you, but these things always take the same sort of form. We'll talk a brief bit about each of the plays, in chronological order, where they came from, how you wrote them –

Yeah, great, I actually love reading these intros. It feels mad doing one of my own.

Why do you love them?

I think it's a place where writers are often quite honest. You get a sense of who they are and what's important to them, from the way they look back at their old plays. And you can pick up some really good tips and bits of advice as a writer!

I'd like to start with *Four Minutes Twelve Seconds*, which was your debut play –

Well, you know what, it wasn't. I actually had a play on in London about four years before. It was called *Lines*, and it probably changed my life more than any included here.

How so?

Well, I started out writing comedy – sketches and stuff – but it never felt natural, like I was wearing clothes that didn't fit and everyone could tell. My first writing partner was Jamie Demetriou, who's an astonishing comedy writer and performer, and I remember sitting across from him as we were working and thinking: 'Fuck. How the hell does he do that?' My brain doesn't work that way.

So how did *Lines* come about?

Around the same sort of time, Tom Martin, who would go on to direct *Ross & Rachel*, pushed me to write him something he could put on in the theatre above The Rosemary Branch pub in Islington. This was in 2010. And I wrote this thing which wasn't funny, but was dramatic and sort of formally playful and it felt like, 'Okay, maybe this is more me than the comedy stuff.' We put it on for a week or so and it was very special for a few reasons. It made me want to be a playwright. It was how I met my agent Emily, who has been with me the entire time. It was also the only play of mine my dad saw performed.

And that led to *Four Minutes Twelve Seconds* –

Four Minutes came a few years later. I got funding to do a writing MA, and in that year I wrote loads and saw loads and I got to know the other brilliant writers on the course. One of them, Vinay Patel, is still one of the few people I share my early drafts with. He'll almost certainly be the only one of my mates who'll read this intro, so I should say hi to him.

I became a complete theatre obsessive during this period. I worked in theatre bars and I reviewed for theatre blogs and I submitted writing to every short play night under the sun. I wrote a lot of plays that I'm very glad never made it to the stage. But you learn, don't you, from each of them, you learn a bit about who you are as a writer.

Is it hot in here?

A bit, yeah.

I shouldn't have worn this jumper. What were we talking about?

Four Minutes…

Right. Yes. How it came about.

My dad had died in spring 2013, and in the months that followed, to distract myself I sort of threw myself into working on an old idea in a frenzy, until it became *Four Minutes Twelve Seconds*. I think I wrote it in May and June of that year, at the small desk in my bedroom in a flat in Shadwell that I shared with four of my best mates.

You've said before that it was inspired by Dennis Kelly's play *Orphans*.

That's a polite way of saying I ripped it off. I remember seeing *Orphans* at the Traverse in Edinburgh and it blew my mind that people were audibly gasping. I love stuff that has twists. I wanted to write something like that.

So I sort of tried on the Dennis Kelly 'style' to see if it fit, and I set it in Croydon, where I grew up. There was so much in the air at the time about toxic masculinity and young men and consent, and they were subjects I wanted to write about. But it's also a play about the nature of justice, I think. I nicked the structure of a detective drama, with Di as the detective, investigating this rumour about her son.

It wasn't initially supposed to go on at Hampstead Theatre, was it?

It wasn't supposed to go on anywhere! I'd sent it round and had some polite 'no thank you's and it was runner-up in a competition, which was more than I'd ever had before. I was really chuffed with that. I had no illusions it would happen because you don't expect plays to ever happen, really, do you?

And then – I remember the phone call so clearly. I was working an office job and I went out into the stairwell and was told that Hampstead had had an issue with a play they had programmed, or something, and suddenly they had a free space in a few weeks with nothing to put on. Was *Four Minutes* still available to fill the gap? Completely insane, lucky break. To me, at that point, it felt like winning the lottery.

I was partnered with Anna Ledwich as a director, who is still one of the best I've ever worked with. It was my dream production. We even cast Jonathan McGuinness, who was in *Orphans* and so had been the voice of David that I'd always imagined in my head. I got to do all these things I'd never done before: the rehearsal process, the model box, the opening night, holding the playtext in my hand. I went almost every night of the run. The actors made fun of me.

And you were working on... (*Coughs.*) Excuse me... on *Ross & Rachel* at the same time?

Yeah, that's right. We started it before, actually. I made it with two good mates, Tom Martin as director and Andy Hughes as producer. We wanted to do something cheap which we could take to Edinburgh, because we figured no one else would put our stuff on.

Did it always have that uh, uh, sorry, that title, and the *Friends* references?

No! It was always about love, and pop culture. I think it always had that form, a two-hander for one actor, but it was originally about a couple who loved rom-coms. It didn't really work, because I was having to do too much to establish the characters before the plot kicked in.

And then at some point it struck me that they shouldn't love rom-coms, they should be *from* a rom-com. I called Tom and asked him what he thought and credit to him, he told me to run with it. Calling your play *Ross & Rachel* instantly does so much legwork for you. You get who these people are.

I've got to ask – is it actually supposed to be them?

It's written so that it could totally be them, but it could also be a couple that happened to be extremely ridiculously similar. Is that diplomatic enough? We spent the entire time worrying about a cease and desist from Warner Bros.

We put it on in an airless shipping container in Edinburgh and it was a hot summer and people kept fainting, which had nothing to do with the content of the show, but we sort of pretended it did. It had this brutal, delicate performance by Molly Vevers, and the play did well and found an audience. That summer will always be one of the best of my life. There's nothing like making something with your friends.

***Four Minutes* and *Ross & Rachel* are quite different beasts, stylistically... Which do you... I'm sorry...**

That's alright. Are you alright?

Which do you... yes... which do you prefer?

Depends! I get jealous of the freedom of some of the choices
I made in *Four Minutes*, because it has that 'early play' thing of
being written on pure instinct that you can never get back. But
Ross & Rachel felt like me stretching my legs for the first time, in
terms of what was allowed. Would you like to move outside? We
could go somewhere else.

No, no I'm fine.

Are you sure?

**Yes, let's keep going. *Parliament Square* feels like you
stretching your legs even more...**

Yeah. It was a bit of a gamble, that one. It came into being when
it won the Judges' Award at the Bruntwood, which is the prize
run by the Royal Exchange in Manchester.

Back then it was always my rule to apply for everything. I had a
little list of deadlines written down, and for years I would send
something in to every competition, every open-submission
window, whatever. Didn't matter what it was. But the Bruntwood
deadline was approaching and I didn't have anything.

**I read that you uh... you wr... wr... wrote it in a couple
days?**

Yes. Well. No. I did and I didn't. I'd written this play called
Trafalgar Square which was about two lovers in a dystopian
future and maybe the only thing interesting about it was there
was a moment of self-immolation. And so when the Bruntwood
deadline came around I thought, 'Okay, I'll nick that image and
I'll start again and really try and get inside the head of someone
who is about to do that.'

I wrote it quickly, over the course of a couple of days in a café
opposite my girlfriend Tam's flat. The play is dedicated to her.
But I'd already laid a lot of the groundwork in writing the other
play, so...

**It sounds like in y... your writing process you start again a
lot...**

It's how I work, really. What I'll often do is – and this is such an
inefficient way of working – I'll write a play and then I'll throw
everything away. Changing the big stuff. The form, the structure,

the story, you know. Again and again until it feels right. I will
often write three or four completely different plays over many
years about the same 'idea' or a character before I work out
which one is the right one. It's very impractical.

Anyway, after the Bruntwood win, the Royal Exchange partnered
me up with Jude Christian as a director, and she and Suzanne
Bell, as dramaturg, helped me develop *Parliament Square* over a
couple of years. And then Jude made this incredible, strange,
intense production.

What are your memories of the production at the Exchange?

It was a wild experience. It was a much bigger stage than I'd ever
worked on. The play was quite divisive. We had a one-star
review! I remember not being able to sleep, re-reading it over and
over. I had this mortifying feeling, like I'd let everyone down
because Sarah Frankcom and Suz at the Exchange had put so
much faith in me and this bit of new writing, by putting it on the
main stage – and it had been slammed. But they were great about
it, and told me not to worry and that they really believed in the
play. Some people loved it and some people hated it. But the
brain always focuses on the people that hated it, doesn't it?

Why do you think it was so divisive?

I think it's quite an ambiguous play. I honestly don't know what
the play is saying about Kat's act of protest.

And of course, you never find out why she's doing it.

That too. I toyed in some drafts with giving her a concrete
reason, but as soon as you do that it becomes more about the
issue than the act itself. There is also a thing where the play is
sort of deliberately anticlimactic –

Where can you go after you set your main character on fire at the end of Act One?

Exactly! And that's exactly the question I was trying to explore.
What happens *after* the life-changing event is over. But that's
anti-theatrical in many ways, I suppose. Because that first act is
seat-of-your-pants stuff and the rest is like a balloon deflating. A
lot of drama schools and universities do it these days, which
I love. It's probably the play of mine I'm most associated with.

After Parliament Square –

I did *Lava.*

Which feels feels quite different.

Yeah. Laura Ford and Angharad Jones, who ran a new-writing company called Fifth Word, commissioned me in 2015 to come up with an idea. It took me years to give them something, and then they trusted it and developed it and developed it and developed it.

There's a lightness to *Lava* that's missing from some of your other plays.

Yeah, that was deliberate. It started life differently, as a sort of angry studio play. The silence was always part of it, but Vin was a much scarier, more violent character, and the other people in his life were more grotesque. It was altogether a weirder, uglier proposition.

Why did did you did you change it? Sorry.

I remember sitting watching *Parliament Square* right before Christmas, and watching the audience's faces as Kat self-immolated and thinking, 'Fucking hell, James. Who wants to watch this just before Christmas? You know? Wouldn't it be nice, if just for once you wrote something with a bit of sunlight?'

I hate to ask, but I don't suppose you have any paracetamol?

I don't unfortunately. I can ask at the counter?

It's just a bit of a headache. I'll pick some up afterwards. Go on –

Anyway, I went away and rewrote *Lava*, this time letting some hope and humour in, and it all fell into place. We did a two-week run in 2018 and it was supposed to tour in 2020, but then Covid hit. By the time it was finally revived in 2022, we were in a different world and the play had grown so much closer to my heart.

Vin and Jamie are two sides of me, I think. That seems obvious to me now, but wasn't when I was writing it. And I think the cat coming back to life at the end of the play is maybe my favourite thing I've ever written.

Why?

Because it's strange. And surprising. And I don't know what it means.

The final play in this collection is *Skyscraper Lullaby*, which was made as an an an audio... drama.

I love audio, I've written quite a few radio plays and it's such a fun medium to write for because you can be really formally bold, you can do what you like. With *Skyscraper* I wanted to write something enormous that could feasibly be done on stage and in audio, in completely different –

Sorry, keep going.

Are you sure? You look, uh...

Yeah I'll just, let me... please, go on.

Okay... It was another reworking of an old idea, a monster play I'd written for Tom and Andy after *Ross & Rachel*. We couldn't get it on anywhere, and so I forgot about it until I got this commission. I decided I would go back to the monster idea, but I was quite burnt out at the time and maybe a bit depressed, and then Covid came along and the pandemic made it worse, and I don't know. I suddenly found that I couldn't write any more.

Not writer's block, exactly, but something was gone. The things I was writing didn't sound like me. I didn't trust my instincts. I couldn't take risks. And so the work dried up. I lost a lot of commissions. I hit dead ends. I forgot everything I liked about the job. And I couldn't finish *Skyscraper* for years.

And then I was flicking through Stephen King's book *On Writing*, which talks really eloquently about stories being found things, like fossils, and that a writer's job is to dig them up without overthinking. And it unlocked something in me again and I started to dig. I sat in this IKEA chair we have, and I just tried to have fun writing this really dark, Stephen King tribute act, with these warring narratives.

And I felt like me again. The relief. I'd love to see a stage production. I have no idea whether the mother or the father's stories are true. I only know that the doctor's story is.

What are some things some things some... (*Coughs a few times.*) What advice do you give to writers starting out?

The first is to not be afraid of rewriting the big things. As I've said, one thing that all these plays have in common is that they started life with completely different forms, different structures, different stories, different titles. They are all the direct descendants of other plays that will never be performed, but had to exist in order to get me to where I needed to be.

The second is to be surprising. It's so nice to be surprised when you're watching or reading something. When it turns into something you didn't expect. A bit of magic.

I'm sorry... I...

Are you sure you're alright? God, you look quite pale.

Yes I just need... can we pause for a second... a... maybe some water

(*To the waiter.*) Hi, sorry, could we get a glass of water, thank you.

Sorry... this migraine...

We don't have to keep going.

No no I just... I need a minute... ah

Take your time.

Thank you... I just need to... ah...

Drink this.

Breathe... And... Oh... Oh? What's that doing there?

What?

I see... is he alright?

Who?

The dog... is he alright...

What dog?

The dog the little dog he's there

Maybe I should call someone.

Are you alright is he tell me tell me are you are you are you you... y... y...

(*The sound of a chair collapsing. Shocked reactions.*)

I... ah... I...

Oh my god call an ambulance, please, please they've collapsed can you quick oh my god call a fucking ambulance

......

....

....

Hi James. Thank you so much for talking to me again.

How long have you been home?

A few weeks now.

I'm so glad to hear it. How's the recovery going?

I'm doing fine. Miraculously. No recurrences, touch wood.

That's great. How are you feeling?

Lucky.

We really didn't have to do this chat, you know.

I wanted to finish the interview. To see if there was anything you wanted to add.

That's really kind of you. Before we start –

Yes?

Can I ask. Just before you collapsed. You saw something over my shoulder. Do you remember it? I'm sorry. I shouldn't pry.

No, it's fine.

You really don't have to –

Yes. I saw something. A hallucination, or

I don't know.

It was

In the air above your shoulder I saw this picture, this painting that used to hang in my office. Just floating in the air in the café. A painting of a little dog's head with its body submerged in something brown and horrible. Water or mud or tar or

And as I was having my seizure, the painting came alive. I could see the little dog, and I knew it was moving but I could only see its head, its sad little head, because the rest of it was submerged under the brown stuff.

And sometimes it looked like it was swimming and sometimes it looked like it was drowning and so I tried to ask it, 'Are you alright, little dog? Are you alright? Which is it? Are you swimming or are you drowning?' – and it turned its little head towards me, but I couldn't tell from his expression.

I couldn't tell if he was keeping his head afloat or was about to slip right under.

And all I wanted was to know.

But the dog just just kept paddling.

Well. I'm just glad you're feeling better.

So. Is there anything else you'd like to add?

Honestly?

I can't think of anything.

FOUR MINUTES TWELVE SECONDS

Four Minutes Twelve Seconds was first performed at Hampstead Theatre Downstairs, London, on 2 October 2014. The cast was as follows:

DI   Kate Maravan
DAVID   Jonathan McGuinness
NICK   Alexander Arnold
CARA   Ria Zmitrowicz

Director   Ann Ledwich
Designer   Janet Bird
Lighting Designer   Mark Howland
Sound Designer   Sarah Weltman
Production Manager   Pam Nichol
Company Stage Manager Robyn Hardy
Deputy Stage Manager   Ashleigh German
Line Producer   Will Mortimer

Characters

DI
DAVID
NICK
CARA

Note

Breaks in text marked by a **...** indicate a jump in time.

Punctuation and spacing are intended as an indication of rhythm, but open to interpretation.

Two parents.

DI	This is Jack's shirt.
DAVID	Yeah.
DI	There's blood down it.
DAVID	There is.
DI	Blood. On his shirt.
DAVID	No flies on you, are there?
DI	Where is he?
DAVID	Now –
DI	Where is he?
DAVID	In his room.
DI	Is he okay?
DAVID	He's fine.
DI	There's blood on his shirt.
DAVID	He had a nosebleed.
DI	It's a nice shirt. A nosebleed?
DAVID	A nosebleed.
DI	No he didn't.
DAVID	How'd you know?
DI	He don't get nosebleeds.
DAVID	Well this time he did. A gusher.
DI	Tell me what happened.
DAVID	A gusher.
DI	Tell me what happened.
DAVID	Diane

DI   David.

DAVID   Do you really want to do this now?

            He was jumped by some lads.

DI   Oh my god.

DAVID   Coming out of school. Nothing serious.

DI   He was fighting?

DAVID   Nothing serious.

DI   He was fighting.

DAVID   He didn't do anything. Says he didn't know them.

DI   Who were they?

DAVID   Says he didn't know them. Some lads from St
            Thomas's. Picking on the posh kids.

DI   He ain't posh.

DAVID   He wears a blazer.

DI   They make him.

DAVID   St Thomas's don't wear a blazer.

DI   And that makes him posh does it?

DAVID   You know what it's like. He's fine. Bloody nose.
            Nothing to write home about.

DI   Nothing to write home about?

DAVID   Worse things happen at sea.

DI   Jack! Come here, would you?

DAVID   Leave him.

DI   I want to see he's alright.

DAVID   He's embarrassed.

DI   Embarrassed? What's he got to be embarrassed about?

DAVID   Well it's embarrassing innit.

DI   You said that to him?

DAVID   No! I would never. But you know.

DI   We should call the police.

DAVID   Come on...

DI   They attacked a schoolboy.

DAVID   He's hardly a schoolboy.

DI   He's seventeen.

DAVID   From what he says they were round the same age. It's kids' stuff.

DI   Don't matter.

DAVID   They'll laugh at you.

DI   The school then. Should at least phone the school.

DAVID   It didn't happen at school.

DI   I mean that was why we sent him there, to get away from this. They'll want to know, they can put measures in –

DAVID   Measures?

DI   Up security. Send a letter round.

DAVID   Just teenagers, innit? Teenagers fight with teenagers. Happened when we were at school, it'll happen when his kids go to school as well. Circle of life.

DI   This ain't *The Lion King*.

DAVID   I know.

DI   It's West Croydon.

DAVID   I'm well aware of that.

DI   Your *son* has been attacked. You might not give two shits –

DAVID   I do give two shits.

DI   You might not give two shits –

DAVID   I give a lot of shits but –

DI   But I do. I knew once he got to this age living round
          here

DAVID   You can't blame the area.

DI   I can blame the area. I can blame the area and I'm
          calling that school and I'm making sure that they do
          something about it. He's my little boy. I don't care
          how old he is.

DAVID   There you go again.

DI   There I go where again?

DAVID   'My *little boy*.' 'My *baby*.' No wonder he's a target.

DI   Just a quick call.

DAVID   It's not a good idea.

DI   Don't know why you're so against this.

DAVID   It's not that.

DI   Is there something I don't know?

DAVID   There's nothing you don't know.

DI   Oh god there's something I don't know. What's
          happened?

DAVID   You're paranoid.

DI   I can always tell.

DAVID   You can never tell.

DI   Your face.

DAVID   What face?

DI   What's wrong?

DAVID   There's nothing wrong. You always say there's
          something wrong when there's nothing wrong but you
          saying something's wrong makes me act like
          something's wrong. There's nothing wrong. I just don't
          think it'll help anyone calling up the school. Jack's fine.

DI   I'm calling them right now unless you give me a
          reason not to.

DAVID   Come on.

DI   I mean it David.

DAVID   Alright. Just. Just put the phone down, for god's sake.

It weren't just some boys from St Thomas's.

DI   Then why'd you say it was?

DAVID   Jack promised me not to say anything. He knew you'd kick off.

DI   I knew it. What's he done?

DAVID   He's not done anything.

DI   But he knows who hit him?

DAVID   Yes.

DI   Who was it?

Who. Was it?

DAVID   If I tell you, you've got to promise not to lose it.

DI   Jesus.

DAVID   Promise me you won't go mental?

DI   Alright.

DAVID   Okay.

It was.

It was Ian.

DI   Ian.

DAVID   That's right.

DI

I have no fucking idea who that is.

DAVID   Yes you do, of course you do. Ian. Cara's brother?

DI   Cara Jack's girlfriend?

DAVID   Yes Cara Jack's girlfriend. What other bloody Cara –

DI   What's Cara's brother –

DAVID	What other Cara could I possibly be –
DI	What's he doing hitting Jack?
DAVID	They broke up.
DI	Hitting anyone of any age for that matter –
DAVID	Did you hear me? They broke up.
DI	Who did?
DAVID	Who d'you think? Jesus Christ.
DI	Jack and Cara? He didn't say. He didn't tell me. Why'd he tell you?
DAVID	I asked.
DI	You asked? He didn't tell me. When'd this happen?
DAVID	Couple of weeks he said.
DI	Well. That's a shock. I'm shocked. That's a shock.
DAVID	I spose.
DI	I mean I'd like to say I saw it coming but no. No, that's definitely a shock. Although I can't say I'm not relieved. Aren't you relieved? I'm quite relieved. I know he was keen on her but she was a bit. What's the word? I'm trying not to be rude.
DAVID	I know what you're trying to say.
DI	You know what I'm trying to say. She was always a bit of a –
DAVID	Doesn't matter now.
DI	I hope he's alright. Is he alright? Did it end badly?
DAVID	I don't know, do I?
DI	And that's why her brother hit him?
DAVID	I can imagine it's got something to do with it.
DI	Hang on. But Ian's Cara's dad's name.
DAVID	And her brother's.
DI	Big Ian called his son Ian?

DAVID   Ian Junior.

DI   Always find that odd.

DAVID   I know.

DI   Specially with a name like Ian.

DAVID   I know.

DI   Isn't Cara's brother in his twenties?

DAVID   He's twenty.

DI   No man in his twenties should be going round hitting
          schoolboys. Just because he broke up with her

DAVID   He didn't. She broke up with him.

DI
          Really?
          No. Really?
          No.

DAVID   That's what he told me anyway.

DI   Not sure who she thinks she is. Not gonna get another
          boy like Jack any time soon, is she...? I mean anyone
          who saw those two together could see it. She was so
          and Jack well he's... So what's Ian-the-brother's
          problem? Mind you that boy that brother well he's
          always been a bit off, hasn't he? Always been
          something a bit I mean Julie's mum said he was one of
          those burnt down Reeves Corner.

DAVID   They caught the bloke that burnt down Reeves.

DI   I spose it's not his fault. I spose who wouldn't be a bit
          messed up coming from that family? That father. Why
          we let Jack get involved with that lot in the first
          place... I said didn't I say when we met that girl.

DAVID   You did. Yes.

DI   Her dad, he was just the same weren't he?

DAVID   You said it several times.

DI   He was awful to you at school.

DAVID   He was alright.

DI   He made your life a misery. I remember.

DAVID   That was a long time ago.

DI   Used to bully you something rotten.

DAVID   Kids' stuff. That's all.

DI   You should call him.

DAVID   Who?

DI   Her dad. Big Ian. Go round there. Tell him what his son's been up to.

DAVID   Look love, I don't think so.

DI   You're mates these days.

DAVID   See him every now and then.

DI   There you go.

DAVID   Down the pub.

DI   There you go.

DAVID   Talk about the kids, mostly.

DI   More than he ever does with me. Stone fucking silence with me. You should call him. Or I should.

DAVID   Oh for –

DI   Maybe I should?

DAVID   Will you please stop trying to call everyone? Just let it be.

DI   He's upstairs with a broken heart and a broken nose –

DAVID   You calling that family up and telling them what's happened is not going to make a blind bit of difference. Trust me. Fact it'll almost certainly make things worse. You know what they're like. Ian –

DI   Ian-the-dad?

DAVID   Ian-the-dad. He'll find it funny.

DI   Funny?

DAVID   Just kids, he'll say. Just leave it alone.

DI   I don't care if he finds it hysterical. His boy's assaulted our boy and it's as simple as that. Where's the number? You must have the number.

DAVID   Don't. I'm serious. You don't need to tell him.

DI   Why not?

DAVID   Because.
Because well. I think he already knows.

The way Jack tells it, Big Ian was there when it happened. In the car. He was waiting in the car while his son collared Jack.

DI   In the car?

DAVID   The way Jack tells it, he was watching. He was shouting his son on. The way Jack tells it, if Ian Junior hadn't got to him first, Big Ian would've done.

DI   You're joking?

DAVID   I'm not.

DI   You're joking?

DAVID   I'm definitely not.

DI   What does he think he's doing? Jack's only seventeen. I mean I knew he was an bit of a thug but this is very serious. It's physical assault. They're grown men. It's physical assault. They assaulted him. It's physical assault.

DAVID   Stop saying physical assault.

DI   I'm telling the police.

DAVID   No.

DI   It's my responsibility. As a mother. And a citizen.

DAVID   A citizen?

DI   What if they're doing this to other boys?

DAVID   You can't call the police.

DI   You what? You want me to do nothing.

DAVID   That's not what I'm –

DI   That man that brute he's been threatening your son
        he's been setting his mental son on our boy and you
        just want me to stand by?

DAVID   You're not listening to me you're not look just settle
        down and listen to me you can't you can't call the
        police.

        Just listen. Please.
        Jack. Right. He made promise me I wouldn't tell you,
        but see

        I know you've got a right to

        So I'm telling you. I want you to remember that.
        I want you to remember that I told you.

DI   What is it?

DAVID   Because I don't want you doing anything stupid before
        you're aware of all the… facts.

DI   Tell me what happened.

DAVID   I didn't want to have to. I mean, Jesus, you're his
        mother.

DI   You're worrying me now.

DAVID   They broke up. Him and Cara.

DI   I know that.

DAVID   But apparently,

DI   You already told me that

DAVID   Apparently there's a bit more to it than that.

        Apparently, well, he says there's a

        There's a video.

DI   A video?

DAVID   A video and it's found its way online.

DI   What sort of video?

DAVID   Online. You know. Apparently it shows
            I mean it's like a film of them

            of Jack and Cara. You know
            and you see...

DI   Oh Jesus.

DAVID   They're in his room. And then

DI   Oh god.

DAVID   That's right.

DI   Why didn't you tell me this?

DAVID   Jack says he don't know how it got online.

DI   A video.

DAVID   He says they only made it for a laugh. On his phone.
            And now somehow it's got out
            And this girl, well she's devastated.

DI   How does something like that get out?

DAVID   I dunno. There are loads of sites with these sort of
            videos.

DI   What was he thinking?

DAVID   So I hear, anyway.

DI   How did they get hold of it?

DAVID   He says a virus maybe. One of these hackers.

DI   What happens?

DAVID   What d'you mean?

DI   In the video. What are they doing?

DAVID   Why d'you want to know that? What possible reason –

DI   Have you seen it?

DAVID   Course I haven't seen it. What d'you take me for?

DI   But anyone can? For free? I feel sick.

DAVID   He tried to get it taken down, he said, but it was too late.

DI   I feel physically –

DAVID   These things are copied, passed around.

DI   How many people?

DAVID   Once they're up, they're up for good.

DI   How many people?

DAVID

Five hundred thousand.

DI   Fucking hell.

DAVID   Only been up a week.

DI   Don't sound proud. Do not sound proud.

DAVID   I didn't. I wasn't.

He says they all do it. These kids, you know, they've got their phones. Film everything. Can't say I blame them. I would at that age. Wouldn't you?

DI   What? No.

DAVID   You would. Course you would. Curiosity. You're young. You want to know what you look like. Don't you? Everyone wonders what they look like when they're…

DI   Do they? I don't.

DAVID   You do. Come on. We've done. In our time. Not that, obviously. But things. Some things. Some very good things.

DI   He's so young.

DAVID   He's seventeen. At his age I was. Well.
Problem is Cara, well, she thinks he put it up deliberately. That he's done it to humiliate her.

DI   Why would he do that?

DAVID   Because she dumped him.

DI   That's ridiculous. He wouldn't do that.
            He wouldn't do that.

DAVID   He swears he never showed it to anyone, never put it
            on the site.

DI   A hacker?

DAVID   He thinks. He thinks a hacker or –

DI   Or?

DAVID   He was hacked. That's probably it.

DI   Who's or?

DAVID   He said he don't know but Nick

DI   Nick.

DAVID   Nick was the last one to use his computer.

DI   Nick Jones or Thick Nick?

DAVID   Thick Nick. Jack doesn't know for sure. It might not
            have been him.

DI   It was him.

DAVID   I mean it probably was him.

DI   Little perv.

DAVID   He thinks maybe when he let him borrow it.

DI   I'm gonna kill him. Don't he realise what he's done?
            That poor girl. And her father knows? Her brother
            knows?

DAVID   You've got to understand, way her dad sees it, way her
            brother sees it…

DI   Jesus.

DAVID   I mean that's their little girl. That's their sister. And
            there's Jack…

DI   What are we going to do? That family…

DAVID   The poor boy's upstairs terrified. He was lucky to get
            away today. He thinks they're gonna kill him.

DI   How could he be so –

DAVID   I know.

DI   Fucking stupid.

DAVID   I know.

DI   We'll have to go round there… convince them that it
          wasn't his fault. That he never meant for the video to
          get out.

DAVID   Only –

DI   Get some some computer genius to have a look and
          show them it was a Nick or a hacker or whatever.
          They're kids. These things happen. They'll understand.

DAVID   Only thing is –

DI   What now? There's nothing more? Tell me there's
          nothing more.

DAVID   You've got to understand. Cara, right now she hates
          his guts. Thinks Jack put up the video. Jack says she's
          trying to get back at him. And to do that, she's told her
          dad and brother, well, she's told them. She's told them
          some things. She's accused Jack of some… things.

DI   Things?

          What sort of things?

DAVID   I think.
          I think you should talk to Jack.

                        …

DI   She's lying.

DAVID   Course she is. She's trying to get back at him. Half the
          world's seen that video.

DI   I could strangle her. Saying something like that. That
          little
          That he would ever dream of forcing anyone to
          Let alone his girlfriend to to
          I mean I can't even say it

        I don't even want to
        This is his life she's playing with.

        We shouldn't have let them have sex in the house.

DAVID   What did he say?

DI   I said didn't I. I said that they were too young. But you had to be Mr Hippy Dad didn't you and now here we are.

DAVID   They were gonna do it somewhere.

DI   They were too young and now look what's happened.

DAVID   It's hardly. I mean we couldn't haven't predicted this.

DI   How could she say that about him. That he would –
He would never. Make a dirty video, okay. He's a teenage boy. I thought better of him but he's a teenage boy. But to accuse him of this. Of –

DAVID   She's angry. She's hurt.

DI   These things stick to a boy. He won't live it down.

DAVID   Quiet.

DI   Everywhere he goes people will think he's a –

DAVID   He'll hear you.

DI   Nobody's gonna believe her are they? I mean he would never. The very idea that he would. Anyone knows Jack knows that he would never.

DAVID   Course they do. Anyone can speak to that. His teachers. His mates. He's never that sort of kid.

DI   And she. Well.

DAVID   No one's gonna believe her.

DI   Her brother believes her.

DAVID   Her brother believes her.

DI   Her psycho brother that tortures fucking cats.

DAVID   He doesn't torture cats.

DI   What were they doing together in the first place?

DAVID   He killed one cat.

DI   What were they doing together? I mean, what did they talk about? She's so. You know. Croydon. Jack's not. He is, obviously. Technically. But he's not. Not really. If that brother –

DAVID   He won't.

DI   He'll have to get away. My sister's.

DAVID   He's not missing school. Not now. With his exams. We keep on as normal.

DI   That boy will kill him. And her dad. You know what her dad's like. If they think this is true –

DAVID   All mouth no trousers with that lot. Always has been. Lot of hot air.

DI   The kid's an arsonist David. Is that what you mean by hot air? He's not right in the head. Jack's staying at my sister's.

DAVID   His exams.

DI   Oh god. What if they call the police?

DAVID   That family? They'd never.

DI   They might.

DAVID   Not in a million years. Prefer to sort things out themselves.

DI   Stupid attitude. My dad was the same.

DAVID   I remember.

DI   Once caught the bloke who nicked my bike.

        Broke two of his fingers.

DAVID   You told me the story.

DI   He was only a kid. Never got the bike back though.

        Fuck.

DAVID   What?

DI   Fuck.

DAVID   What?

DI   We've got dinner at Sue and Peter's tonight.

DAVID   No.

DI   We're sposed to have dinner.

DAVID   Cancel.

DI   I can't cancel.

DAVID   Just call them up

DI   I can't cancel I cancelled before.

DAVID   I'm not going. I'm putting my foot down and I'm not going.

DI   You are going.

DAVID   Shit.

DI   We'll go. We'll go and we'll leave all this alone for a few hours.
          It'll be good to see her.

...

DI   Fucking Sue. I should've slapped her.

DAVID   Calm down.

DI   The hell she think she is talking 'bout my kid

DAVID   Calm down. Just ignore her.

DI   Like her son's so perfect. Like her son's so perfect. She don't even know what happened. She don't even know Cara and she's taking her side that lying little is this what it's gonna be like will people just believe her will people always think he's

DAVID   No.

DI   Because I can't take that. I really can't take that.

DAVID   No course not. It'll die down. You know what they're like.

DI   I mean why is she so quick to think Cara's the one
        telling the truth. Because she's a girl? Fucking Sue
        feminist fucking I tell you if she knew her if she knew
        what Cara was like

DAVID   I said.

DI   What?

DAVID   I did say we shouldn't go.

                        ...

DAVID   Where's my razor? You seen my razor?

DI   What if we called them?

DAVID   Who?

DI   The police. Tell them what's going on.

DAVID   You're joking.

DI   Tell them they attacked Jack, tell them she's been
        spreading lies about him.

DAVID   You can't be serious?

DI   I don't see why not. Get out in front of it. Call her
        bluff. If we don't they'll only go after him again. You
        know they will. If we call the police they might be
        able to do something. Keep him safe. She's lying.
        They'll see that straight away and put a stop to it.

DAVID   We can't put him through that. Not now.

DI   They might even be able to find out how the video got
        out there. Whether it was Nick, or someone else.

DAVID   How would they know that?

DI   They could look at his computer. They can trace these
        things these days, that's how they catch these people.
        Predators and that.

DAVID   If we go to the police about this they'll bring him in.
        Don't you see? They'll go and they'll talk to her and
        you think she's gonna change her story? Not a chance.

They'll back her into a corner and she'll tell them
exactly what she's been telling everyone else, that Jack
forced her into and you know what they'll believe her.
Course they will. And then forever it's on the record
he was accused of I mean they might even charge him.
They might even charge him. You don't want that do
you? Not now, not when he's worked so hard when
he's so close he's so close to doing so well. I mean say
goodbye to uni, to a career, everything. Over what?
A stupid video. No.
No. We keep the police out of it.

DI   So what then? We can't just sit around. Not while
          everyone we know is –

DAVID   Let's just worry about Jack, for now eh? Tonight we'll
          take him to your sister's, sit him down and tell him it's
          all gonna be fine, tell him that everybody knows he
          never uploaded that video and he would never lay a
          finger on that girl.
          No one's gonna believe her. Don't worry. The
          important thing is not to do anything rash. Me and
          you, eh? Right now, it's all just words.

          Where's that fucking razor?

                            ...

DI   Another pint Nick?

NICK   I'm alright.

DI   I don't mind.

NICK   No. Er. No thank you.

DI   Not like you to turn down a free pint.

NICK   I got homework.

DI   What homework?

NICK   General studies.

DI   General studies? What d'you do in general studies?

NICK   Fuck-all actually.

Sorry. They make me do it.

DI   They don't make Jack.

NICK   Top sets don't have to.

DI   You enjoy general studies?

NICK   Where's Jack?

DI   He's not coming.

NICK   Right.

DI   That a problem?

NICK   Er.

DI   I just want a chat with you Nick. That's all. How many times you been round our house eh? Part of the furniture. Every time I come home, there you are, lying on my couch like a big slug. In fact I think this might be the first time I've seen you sitting upright. Almost didn't recognise you. It's alright if it's just us for now, isn't it?

NICK

            Yeah. No. You said Jack was coming is all.

DI   He's gone away for a bit. Staying with my sister.

NICK   Right. Yeah. Course.

DI   Course?

NICK   Just we didn't see him at school so…

DI   You been to this pub before?

NICK   Few times, yeah.

DI   Still a good place to get served, is it? Always used to come here after school. Couldn't've been more than fifteen. Jack's got to use his fake ID now. You got a fake ID?

NICK   Er… yeah.

DI   Says you're eighteen?

NICK   Twenty-seven. More believable.

DI   Used to have a big dog in here you know.

NICK   Oh yeah?

DI   Big slobbery Alsatian. Used to sit right in the middle of the pub so you had to step over it to get to the bar. Bit my mate Jo on the ankle once, when she trod on its foot. Teeth went right to the bone.

NICK   I don't know nothing you know.

DI   I'm sorry?

NICK   About Jack and Cara. I know that's why you brought me here.

DI   You're a clever boy Nick. Anyone ever tell you that?

NICK   First I heard of it was at school. Don't know nothing about the video.

DI   But you've seen it?

NICK   What?

DI   You've seen it though, haven't you? The video. You must've... The whole school must have watched it. Don't worry, I don't mind.

NICK   I... they were playing it in ICT but I didn't look.

DI   Course you didn't.

NICK   I don't wanna see that. Believe me.

DI   Is it true everyone does it?

NICK   Er.

DI   That's what I've been told. That you all do this. Make these videos. Pass them around.

NICK   No. I mean. Some people. Obviously. I don't.

DI   Oh you don't?

NICK   No. I've never.

DI   Because you're too respectful of women?

NICK   Dunno.

DI	Or cos no one will have sex with you?
NICK	I just. I've never. That's all.
DI	How d'you think those girls feel Nick?
NICK	Dunno. Some of them like it.
DI	They like it?
NICK	Some of them, yeah. Some of them send them round themselves.
DI	You're good mates with Cara, aren't you?
NICK	What d'you mean?
DI	I've seen you. When you've both been round. You get on. She likes you.
NICK	So?
DI	How d'you think she feels, knowing half the world's seen her like that? Knowing most of the boys she knows spend their ICT classes laughing at her and their evenings wanking over her?
NICK	She... I ain't spoken to her.
DI	Is there something you want to tell me?
NICK	You what?
DI	I'm not angry.
NICK	Dunno what you're on about.
DI	We know it was you Nick.
NICK	Know what was me.
DI	You uploaded the video from Jack's computer.
NICK	No I never.
DI	And I want you to know we're not cross. We're not. I know you might think we would be. I know you might think that we'd be angry that you used our son's laptop and got your pervy little kicks from invading his privacy.
NICK	I didn't do nothing.

DI   I know you might think I'd want to chop your little cock
        off and feed it to the dogs for a thing like that. Or maybe
        just report you to the police, let them deal with you, like
        you deserve. But I don't. I don't want to do any of that.
        Because all I want from you is to tell the truth.

        Cara's brother. You hear what he did to Jack?

NICK   Course I heard.

DI   And I bet you've heard what Cara's been saying about
        him?

NICK   Yeah.

DI   I'm sorry?

NICK   Yeah. I heard.

DI   They want to kill him Nick. They want to kill him
        because they think he assaulted their little girl. Their
        little sister. And the only reason they think he did is
        because she told them that he did. And the reason she
        told them that he did is because she thinks he uploaded
        the video. Do you see where I'm going with this?

NICK   I don't know what Jack told you –

DI   Talk to Cara, Nick. He's your mate. I know you don't
        want him hurt. Talk to Cara. Tell her it was you.

NICK   It wasn't me.

DI   Tell her you made a mistake, and you'll make it up to
        her, you'll do whatever you can but that her family,
        they've got to leave Jack alone, because he never did
        anything, he never did anything cos he cared about her.

NICK   Fuck off.

DI   Excuse me?

NICK   Fuck off he cared about her. I didn't upload the video,
        alright?

DI   Please Nick. I need your help on this.

NICK   Like I told you. I've not even seen it. I don't want to.
        The thought makes me –

DI   I don't want him hurt.

NICK   And them pictures. I never asked him to send them.
            I told him. I would never.

DI   What pictures?

NICK   Why would I want to see that? Why would I want to
            see her like that?

DI   What pictures Nick?

NICK   I never asked him to.

DI   He sent you pictures of Cara?

NICK   Yeah. Sometimes.

DI   What sort of pictures?

NICK   Only a few. Nothing too bad. Listen, I didn't even look
            at them properly.

DI   Why would he do that?

NICK   Dunno, do I? Ask him.

DI   You're lying.

NICK   Fine.

DI   What were they of?

NICK   I told you, didn't I? Cara. With her top off sometimes.
            Posing. Smiling.

DI   She knew he was taking them?

NICK   She was looking at the camera.

DI   I don't believe you.

NICK   S'what lads do.

DI   He wouldn't.

NICK   Get a good photo, they show it around.

DI   If he sent you these photos then where are they?

NICK   You really wanna see?

DI   No. I. Yes.

NICK   There.
          Jack knew I didn't want to see them. Sent them anyway.

DI   That's enough.

NICK   You asked.

DI   So what? He sent you these photos and you liked the
          look of them so first chance you got you took his
          laptop and went looking for more?

NICK   No.

DI   And you found something better. You found a video.

NICK   No! I never. I wouldn't. I think Cara's… she don't
          don't deserve that.
          She's proper funny. People think she's thick but she's
          not. She's smart. Smarter than I am.

DI   Smart and funny. Right. That's why you watch that
          video.

NICK   I never. Watched it.

DI   I need you to talk to her.

NICK   I keep telling you I didn't post it. I don't care about
          that stuff. Know I'm supposed to but I don't. Yeah
          she's fit really fit but that's not why I like her. I met
          her on the one-oh-nine. Thought she was fascinating.

          And then Jack started going out with her. Sending me
          photos.

DI   Jack could get hurt here Nick. The things she's saying.

NICK   I know what she's saying. Don't you get it? I'm sorry
          but, last thing I'd ever do is tell Cara I uploaded that
          video. I never did it. And I can't have her think I did
          neither. I don't want Jack getting hurt, course I don't but

          Look I don't know if he put that video up there or if
          Cara's telling the truth or what. I hope he didn't and if
          he says he didn't then you should probably believe
          him.

But if you got to choose between him putting it up and me putting it up then you should know that I love her. I really really love her. I think she's the best person in this whole fucking city. And he don't.

He never did. In the video they say –

DI   What?

NICK   Nah.

DI   What do they say?

NICK   They're saying he puts his hand over her mouth. Through the whole thing he puts his hand over her mouth. Like this.

          I gotta go. Cheers for the drink.

          Listen. If you see her. If you talk to her. Don't tell her I've seen those pictures? Please. I gotta go.

...

DAVID   I stopped over to see Jack.

DI   How was he?

DAVID   Tired. Scared.

DI   I'll get over there tomorrow.

DAVID   Sick of your sister. He wants to come home.

DI   You remember when we went to Brighton?
          Before he was born?

DAVID   Brighton?
          Course what about it?

DI   I was wondering –

DAVID   Course I remember.

DI   You still got those photos?

DAVID   Of Brighton?

DI   We took some. You remember. Of me. In the hotel.

DAVID   Oh. Blimey. Those photos.

DI   You still got them?

DAVID   Why d'you ask?

DI   I was just thinking about them about when we took
        them and I wondered –

DAVID   Remember hiding them pretty well when Jack got old
        enough to find things.
        Didn't want him seeing those. Scar him for life seeing
        you in some of those positions.
        I can look in the loft.

DI   Did you ever show them to anyone?

DAVID   You what?

DI   Back then. Or since. Round the pub or something.

DAVID   Why you asking this?

DI   Don't mind if you did I'm just

        interested.

DAVID   He didn't upload the video. Jesus.

DI   I know.

DAVID   It was Nick. You know that.

DI   Nick. Yeah.

        I went to see him actually.

DAVID   You're kidding.

DI   Met him for a drink.

DAVID   Jesus Christ.

DI   Well I had to do something.

DAVID   I thought we agreed.
        Nothing rash we said.

DI   I'm sorry.

DAVID   Well.
        What did he say?

DI   He says he didn't do it.

DAVID   There's a surprise.

DI   I really went for him.

DAVID   I should hope so.

DI   I mean I said don't he know the trouble he's got Jack
in. Could've smacked him there and then. I wanted to.

DAVID   You should've.

DI   But he kept talking.

DAVID   Been well within your rights.
You know the more I think about it the more I ought to –
Don't know. Go see him myself.
Have a word.

DI   A word?

DAVID   You know what I mean. Sort him out.

DI   Sort him out? He's a teenager.

DAVID   Old enough.

DI   Come on. You've never done that to anyone in your
life.

DAVID   I have. Course I have.

DI   Who?

DAVID   What d'you mean who? Loads of people. Back in the
day.

DI   It's alright.

DAVID   Back in the day.

DI   Come off it. You've never been like that. That's why
I love you.

DAVID   I'm going round.

DI   You're not going round. He's a child and you've got
high blood pressure. What's got into you? I don't like
you like this.

DAVID   Well, after what he did.

DI   That's the thing.
            I don't think it was Nick.

DAVID   Course it was.

DI   He says he's in love with Cara.

DAVID   What?

DI   That's what he says.

DAVID   Bollocks.

DI   That's what he says. He says he's in love with her. Said
            it quite sweetly actually. Says he met her first, on the
            bus. Before Jack. Says he thought she was fascinating.

DAVID   Fascinating?

DI   That's the word he used.

DAVID   And he's talking about Cara?
            I mean she's a lot of things but –

DI   But then Jack started going out with her instead.

DAVID   Well. Luck of the draw innit. I mean, can you blame
            her?

DI   He's heartbroken. I thought he might cry.

DAVID   His best mate's girlfriend. He cried?
            Well it's obvious what's happened, innit? He's obsessed.

DI   I don't know.

DAVID   Explains why he uploaded it.

DI   I dunno. Would you want to see that? Your best mate
            and the girl you like. He says he hasn't even watched
            it. Can't think of anything worse.

DAVID   We should tell Jack. He deserves to know.

DI   Nick said –

            Never mind.

            Apparently in the video. The whole way through. Jack.
            He keeps his hands his hands over her mouth.

DAVID   You what?

DI   While they're... he keeps his hand on her mouth the whole time. He said.

DAVID   Oh. Well that doesn't mean –

DI   Of course not.

DAVID   That could be anything.

DI   I know. It could be, right?

DAVID   I mean, I've done that to you. Before.

DI   Yeah. You have. No I know.

    That doesn't mean anything. Does it?

...

DI   Those photos.

DAVID   This again.

DI   You really never showed them to anyone?

DAVID   Of course not. You're my wife.

DI   Then what were they for?
    If you never wanted to show them to anyone –

DAVID   Because you were gorgeous. You still are.
    I dunno, do I? A memento.
    We were in a hotel. It was sexy. Christ, it was twenty years ago.

DI   We never look at them.

DAVID   You want to look at them? If you want to look at them I can check in the loft.

DI   It's fine.

DAVID   I don't mind. It might be nice.

DI   Jack's been taking photos of Cara. Sending them round.

DAVID   You what?
    Who told you that?

DI   Sending them to his mates.

DAVID   I can't believe –

DI   Nick showed me. Showed me some Jack sent him.

DAVID   He showed you?

DI   It wasn't too bad.

DAVID   What the hell's he doing showing you?

DI   I didn't believe him. I was trying to understand

DAVID   Even so.
            Okay, Jack's been a bit of an idiot.
            I'll talk to him. It doesn't mean.

DI   No. No course not.

DAVID   It doesn't mean he put the video up.

DI   No course not. But it would make sense.

DAVID   Don't say that.

DI   I'm not saying that he definitely put the video up but it
            would make sense. We already know Nick didn't do it.

DAVID   We don't know.

DI   And I think we've gotta be honest that there's a chance
            a very real chance it was Jack. I want to believe him of
            course I do but if he's doing this, if he's sending
            photos like this then it's not a huge leap to think

            Don't you think?

DAVID   I dunno. Maybe.

            It still don't change it. If it was him uploaded it. It still
            don't change that what that girl is saying he did is
            totally out of line.

DI   Maybe if he owns up to it, if he goes to her and says
            he's sorry she'll stop saying what she's saying. Get her
            brother to back down.
            I don't understand it. This impulse to share everything.
            Why would he want that getting out?

DAVID   We don't know for sure.

DI   If you got caught watching something like that when when we were young you were a dirty old man.

Now, it's what? It's normal? They're kids. Two kids having sex helping half a million people toss themselves off. No wonder she's lying through her teeth to get back at him. If I thought someone had done that to me...

But to go this far.
To say that he

And in a strange way it's a relief I'm a bit relieved because if Jack did I mean if he did actually upload the video of them having then it just shows that she's lying about you know.
About the other thing.
Because. Because if you did you know, if you did force someone into
I mean do something like that
even by accident or
and it was on tape then the last thing you'd ever want to do is share it, innit? The last think you'd ever want to do is share it.

Which shows she's lying. I mean I knew she's lying of course I knew she was lying but it shows she's lying. You don't share something like that.

...

DAVID   I've been thinking.

DI   What time is it?

DAVID   About Cara

DI   You been up all night?

DAVID   We can't have her thinking that Jack... that he uploaded the video. Because as long as she thinks that then she's going to keep trying to get back at him and she's gonna keep saying, keep accusing him of these things. And we need him home soon. He's already missed too much school.

I saw her brother in town the other day. Saw him and his mates. Thought they were coming after me. Turns out they weren't. Walked straight past me. Couldn't stop I couldn't stop shaking.

DI   You didn't tell me.

DAVID   We've got to get him home. Put an end to all this. I thought you could maybe go and see her maybe talk to her sort of woman to woman and maybe see how she is. Try and calm her down.

DI   Really? I don't know.

DAVID   I thought you could go and you could convince her that you know, you know who uploaded the video and

DI   How would I know that?

DAVID   I thought you could and hear me out I thought you could maybe tell her and this is this, you know tell me if you think this is stupid, but I thought you could tell her that it was

Me. Maybe. Thought you could tell her that it was me. I mean it wasn't. It wasn't me. And the more I think about it the more I think that maybe you were right maybe Jack did.

But I thought, to get her to back down, to get her to stop punishing him you could tell her I'd done it. Because she'll believe that, see, because if you tell her it was Nick or a virus or whatever else she'll just think you're lying just trying to protect him. But if you go to her and you tell her that it was your husband that did it, and I'm ashamed and I dunno you're gonna stick me in counselling or something well she's gotta believe that, hasn't she?

Cos you see it don't matter if she hates me. It don't matter if they come for me. Just so long as she leaves Jack alone. And her family, they leave Jack alone. Because he hasn't done anything. And he's got his exams.

What you reckon?

DI	No.
DAVID	No?
DI	I'm not doing that.
DAVID	It was just an idea.
DI	It's a fucking awful idea. Really, one of your worst.
DAVID	Oh.
DI	I'm not having people think of you like that. It's sweet it's so sweet of you to want to protect him and we will, we will but there's other ways.
DAVID	Right. Yeah. Yeah.
DI	I love you, you daft prick. I could never live with myself, letting the world think that. Maybe. Maybe you're right though. I should talk to Cara.
DAVID	Yeah? What will you What you gonna say?

...

CARA	You shouldn't be here.
DI	Listen to me.
CARA	You shouldn't be here. You shouldn't be talking to me. Got nothing to say to you.
DI	Just listen to me, Cara, just for a second. Please.
CARA	I'll call my dad.
DI	I just want to talk to you.
CARA	Fuck you.
DI	D'you know what this is doing to Jack? Your brother –
CARA	I'll smack you.
DI	See what happens.
CARA	I'll scream. I'll scream for help and then you'll be fucked.

DI   Just tell me. Tell me why. Look I know you're
          embarrassed. Scared, even. Your dad and and your
          brother –

CARA   Why'd I be scared of them?

DI   Jack says –

CARA   Jack says? Fuck you.

DI   I know you think he put that video up.

CARA   Leave me alone.

DI   But he didn't. He swears he didn't.

CARA   Yeah? Who did then?

DI   It was. It was Nick.

CARA   You think I'm stupid.

DI   So you can go and you can tell your brother and your
          dad

CARA   Nick wouldn't do that.

DI   Tell them that Jack had nothing to do with it and you
          can stop these lies.
          Will you do that Cara?
          I don't know what went on between you two or why
          you split up but to say the things you're saying, don't
          you see? You know, we could talk to them, if you like,
          we could tell your dad –

CARA   What's it got to do with them?

DI   I thought. If you like. Tell your brother –

CARA   Got nothing to do with them.
          You're sick in the head.

DI   I let you into my home. Cooked you dinner.

CARA   Cooked me dinner?

DI   Gave you and Jack your privacy.

CARA   Your cooking's shit.

DI   Nobody believes you, you know that?

CARA   I care?

DI   No one believes a word. You look ridiculous.

CARA   I'm going now. Bye.

DI   Please. Wait.

CARA   Don't touch me.
         I said don't touch me.

DI   It's not a joke. Cara.

CARA   Who's joking?

DI   Your brother –

CARA   Why you keep talking about my brother?

DI   He attacked Jack. Did you know that?

CARA   So?

DI   We're worried about what he's gonna do next. He's
         not going to do anything else is he?

CARA   Fuck should I know? I don't know what he does.

DI   He's only doing this cos you're lying. Jack's terrified.
         He's hiding.

         Please. I'm begging you. Stop saying these things.
         Call off your brother. This is Jack we're talking about.

CARA   You finished?

DI   You know better than anyone what he's working
         towards. His potential.

CARA   His potential?
         Fuck you.

DI   But you've got to stop saying what you're saying
         because the more it gets out look I know how
         embarrassed you must be feeling –

CARA   Embarrassed? You think I'm doing this cos I'm
         embarrassed?

DI   It must be so difficult having something so… personal
         out there. I get it. I do.

CARA   All those people watching? Laughing. Everyone I know.

DI   But he swears he didn't put it up. And even, god forbid, even if he did. And I'm not saying he did. But if he did. It's a mistake.

CARA   I don't care.

DI   A stupid schoolboy mistake, that's all. He doesn't deserve to be punished. Not like this, anyway.

CARA   You really don't get it –

DI   These accusations you're throwing around. You probably don't realise but they stick with a person. They could be with him for the rest of his life. Don't you understand? So whether he uploaded it or –

CARA   Listen to me. Watch my mouth. I. Don't. Care. I don't care if he uploaded it or not. That ain't what this is about.

DI   You're lying.

CARA   Think that if you like. I don't care. But watch that video. Everyone else has. You watch it. You see.

        The rest of his life? He shouldn't give a fuck about the rest of his life.

        He should care about tomorrow and what my brother's gonna do when he finds him.

...

DI

...

DAVID   I can't believe you

DI   Wasn't easy to find. Was looking for an hour. More maybe.

DAVID   You watched it? You watched the video.

DI   There's so much of it out there.

DAVID   Why on earth would you

DI   I mean you hear don't you, of course you know it's
          there

DAVID   Why would you do that to yourself.

DI   But until you actually go looking. There's so much.
          All the same. These videos. All of them.

          Took ages to find the right one. Just kept clicking
          through. Thought I'd found it once or twice but they
          just. It was people that looked like them.
          Video after video after video and then suddenly
          halfway down the page there they were. Actually
          I didn't even see them at first, you can't really, not in
          those little photos they have as the links. But
          I recognised Jack's bedroom. I saw his posters.

DAVID   I don't know why you'd –

DI   When you watch it at first you can't really tell.

          But then if you look closely.

DAVID   Stop it.

DI   If you look at her face. I think you should watch it.

DAVID   I don't understand this. What exactly did she say to you?

DI   I still think of him as nine years old.
          In the video –
          You still haven't seen it?

DAVID   No. No course not.

DI   In the video. If you watch the video well. You can see –

          He grabs her and kisses her and then they're on the bed
          and it looks like it really looks like she doesn't want to.

DAVID   No it doesn't.

DI   He does. He pins her down and puts. He puts his hand
          over her mouth.

DAVID   You shouldn't have watched it.

DI   Puts his hand right on her mouth.

DAVID   It's not like that. I mean I'm sure it's not like that.

DI   Anyone watching can see. I'm amazed no one else has
called the police.
We've got to talk to him.
You haven't seen it

DAVID   So?

DI   You haven't seen what he does so how can you –

DAVID   That's got nothing

DI   How can you know

DAVID   That's got nothing to do

DI	DAVID
Without watching it you can't know. You've not seen. What he does the way he treats her what he does with his hands. You haven't seen it. You haven't seen what he does.	with it. I do. I do know. I know that it's not what you think, you're not seeing what you think, so just calm you're not listening to me just calm down because

DAVID   I have.

         Listen. Alright.

         I have.
         I've watched it.

         I have. Listen. Alright.

         I have.
         I've watched it.

DI   When?

DAVID   Does it matter?

DI   Not on his computer. He deleted it.

         You went looking for it online? When?

DAVID   Why's it matter? You did. What's important is I've
seen it and.

DI   And it doesn't concern you?

DAVID   And I just don't think you're seeing what you think that you're seeing.

DI   What am I seeing?

DAVID   It's just, I know it might look, you know. I know that on camera it might look but from what he says.

DI   I know what he says.

DAVID   From what I can see –

DI   The way he treats her. The way he grabs her. His hand on her mouth.

DAVID   It's a bit rough but it's no worse than –

DI   Than what? Than how we have sex?

DAVID   Than half the videos out there. But yeah. Yeah alright. I think if you watched a video back of us. Not that we would ever. But sometimes. You'd be surprised.

DI   Half the videos out there? How many have you seen?

DAVID   I don't know. Not many. A few.

DI   Jesus.

DAVID   Not often. Just sometimes.

DI   And it's very different from our sex –

DAVID   I don't know.

DI   It's very different.

DAVID   All I'm saying is that things can look strange on camera. When you don't know what's going on. And I don't think that we should jump to. It hardly goes on long enough to tell anyway. Four minutes and it cuts out. It could all be perfectly innocent.

DI   Except she's saying that it's not.

DAVID   How many times? She's lying. And the 'hand on the mouth' thing

DI   I can't believe you watched it.

DAVID   They're trying to keep quiet. That's all. He didn't want us hearing.

DI   He didn't want us hearing?

DAVID   You know what it's like. You remember, at your dad's house. We'd be so quiet.

DI   Bet you'd love to do a video like that.

DAVID   Come on. I would never.

DI   Only cos you couldn't work the camera.
You didn't tell me that you watched it. You let me go on thinking –

DAVID   I. Why'd you think?
I wanted to know what happened. Like you. I wanted to know what went on.

DI   You lied to me.

DAVID   Not exactly.

DI   I used to be able to tell when you were lying.

...

DI   Please. I don't want to fight.

CARA   I gotta be somewhere.

DI   I watched the video.

CARA   And?

DI   I'm… it's… Are you okay? Has anyone asked you that?

CARA   You what?

DI   Just in all of this, in everything with Jack and your dad and your brother and everything. Has anyone actually asked you if you're okay?

CARA   What d'you want?

DI   Just… I don't know really.

CARA   Where's Jack been?

DI   He's gone away.

CARA   Not seen him. Not heard from him.

DI   He's frightened.

CARA   What's he been saying? He said anything 'bout me?

DI   I. I haven't spoken to him.

CARA   Yeah?

DI   Not since he went away.

CARA   Why not?

DI   What happened that night Cara?

CARA   You know what happened.

DI   What was said. Before. After. What made you tell your family that he…

        I know it's hard but I need you to tell me exactly.

CARA   I ain't got to tell you anything.

DI   Please. I need to understand.

CARA   What don't you understand?

DI   He's my son. He was nice to you. Wasn't he?

CARA   Nice? I can't sleep because I keep going over it in my head. Nice? Every time I hear the song that was playing on the radio when he did it I have to hold my breath to stop from throwing up.
        And I know you don't wanna believe that and I know a lot of people aren't gonna believe that but well that's life, innit.

DI   Why then. Why don't the police know? If that's true why haven't you said anything?

CARA   You joking? My dad'd kill me. Anyway, that don't even matter. If I went to them and told them what happened, looking like I do, talking like I do, and then Jack went and he told them what happened, who they gonna believe? Not worth the bother. But my dad. He believes me. And my brother. He believes me. And that's enough.

You want to *understand*? You want to see what your son is?

...

DI   Where have you been?

DAVID   I was.

I stopped by the pub. The Ship of Fools.

Always have to walk past the door when I'm coming from the station. Was passing just now when I saw him. Ian Senior. Sat in the window with a couple of mates.

Stood and watched for a bit, he was saying something and his mates were laughing, and I just thought, something inside me just went. Fuck it. Can't go that badly. Not if they're all laughing. I mean you said right when this all started I should speak to him. Reason with him. Got to do something. Got to say something. So I rapped on the glass to get his attention.

D'you see this? It's actually – look he's ripped it. Not even at the buttons, down the material. That's strong material. D'you realise the force that's taken to rip material like that? Barely got a word out before he went for me. Shouldn't have said anything. Barely got out of there alive.

She was there too, you know. Cara. Bold as brass, as always.

Before I knew it they had me up against the wall. Somehow, I don't know how, but somehow I got free and was able to get across the road back into the station. Thank Christ they didn't follow me in. Sat and waited on the platform until I was sure they'd gone. Could've been thirteen again, pissing myself as him and his mates chased me down the bus stop.

Still. I tried to do something, though. You can't say I didn't try

DI   She's telling the truth.

DAVID   What
          What's the matter with you?

DI   She showed me bruises. Bruises he gave her. Bruises
          from that video.

DAVID   I mean. She could've got those anywhere. Done them
          herself. Jesus. I could've been seriously hurt here.

          Is that –

          Jesus. Are those Jack's emails?

DI   You should read them.

DAVID   What are you doing? You shouldn't be –

DI   Read them. Or I can tell you what they say.

DAVID   I'm not comfortable with this. We shouldn't be doing
          this. If Jack…

          What am I supposed to be –

DI   He did it.

DAVID   Now hang on. Let me –

DI   He did it. It's obvious.

DAVID   You're jumping to conclusions.

DI   Why would he write that to her?

DAVID   Well… I dunno. There could be loads of reasons.

DI   Why would he say those things?

DAVID   Loads of reasons.

DI   What are we going to do?

DAVID   Calm down. This doesn't change anything. No one's
          seen these. I'm sure they're not what they look like.

DI   We can't just do nothing. Pretend we haven't seen
          them.

DAVID   That's exactly what we're going to do. You shouldn't
          have even been looking –

DI   We've got to tell him that we know. That we've seen
          the video. That we've read them.

DAVID   He'd never talk to us again.

DI   We can't just let him –

DAVID   Listen to you. Listen to what you're saying. He's looked
          me in the eyes and he's sworn to me that he didn't do it,
          that that girl is lying. And the very fact that you could
          It sickens me. It does. Hacking into his emails into his
          personal private –
          Hang on. Cara's got these?

DI   Yes.

DAVID   She told you about them.

DI   Yes.

DAVID   Well is she going to the police?

DI   No.
          At least, she says she isn't.

DAVID   Thank god.

DI   Says she don't think they'd believe her. It's like you
          said. That family'd never.

DAVID   Thank god. Well that's something.

DI   But I've been thinking. I've been doing a lot of
          thinking and I think the best thing for us to do. The
          best thing for Jack is.
          I want us to talk to them.

DAVID   Her family?

DI   The police.

DAVID   You're joking.

DI   Show them these emails. Get them to watch the video.

DAVID   Can't believe I'm hearing this.

DI   They can do the rest. Talk to Jack. Talk to Cara.

DAVID   You want to call the police? Over what? You don't
          even know what you're saying.

DI   Sort the whole thing out. Because we, we can't. And
            Cara's family.
            Just look what her dad did to you. Someone will get
            hurt.
            We'll sit Jack down and we'll tell him our reasons.

DAVID   Let's just calm down.

DI   It's our fault. We got him wrong. Don't you see?
            We should never have allowed him to get to the place
            where he could do something like this.

DAVID   Something like what? We don't know for sure that he's
            done anything.

DI   If he hasn't done anything then we've got nothing to
            worry about. But if he has, well –
            If he has

DAVID   If he has well, so what? So. What.

            Not so what.
            I didn't mean so what. Of course, it's bad.
            If he has. If she's telling the truth. Course it's bad. But
            you've seen that video. She was his girlfriend. It's not
            like it's a proper you know.
            And I'm not even saying that it is, that he does, but if
            if it is what she says it is then surely we agree that

DI   What?

DAVID   You know. There are worse. Worse ways. I'm getting
            my words. This is just a a misunderstanding is what
            I'm trying to say. Maybe.
            What I'm trying to say is he's a good kid. He might've
            and I'm saying might here because I still don't believe
            he did but he might've made a mistake. And even if he
            did, he don't deserve this.

DI   I'm his mum. I can't let him think that nothing
            happens to people who do this

DAVID   Who do what?

DI   Because then. Then he'll be that person for the rest of his
            life. I've seen him do it. I've watched him hurt that girl.

DAVID   You only think you have.
         I saw two kids. Two kids playing around.

DI   I'm calling the police.
         I'm sorry.

DAVID   No. No. I will not let you do this.
         I'll stop you. I'm warning you. I will. I don't want to
         have to say this love but if you pick up that phone
         I will be forced to stop you

DI   Stop me? I'm sorry? Stop me how?

DAVID   Why'd we send him to that school eh?

         Please. Just.

         I don't know what went on, and maybe that girl's
         telling the truth and maybe he did what she says he did
         and she's probably hurting but you know what? I don't
         care. I don't care, and I know that's awful, and I know
         that might sound selfish but I don't care because I'm
         not her father I'm his father and I can be as selfish as
         I fucking well like. Let her family worry about her.

         You think he's the only kid to get caught up in
         something like this? Hundreds of thousands of those
         videos go up every day. It's what happens. Sex for them
         is so much more than it ever was when we were his age,
         and I'm not saying that makes it right or that it excuses
         anything but I'm saying that the world is different now.

         He's a good lad. You know that. And you know he
         could be he's got it in him to be somebody really
         fucking great. All that love and care and time and
         effort and money that we've given him, that we've
         both put into making him the person we want him to
         be. I will not let one stupid one stupid mistake take
         that away from me. From him. He's my son, and I love
         him more than more than even you maybe and I'm
         sorry but I won't, I won't let his life be ruined before
         it's even begun.

         D'you understand?

I can't let you do that. Not over a stupid fucking video.

DI   Did you upload it?

DAVID   What?

DI   I've been thinking. I keep thinking why you'd sit up sit up half the night and then you'd tell me to tell Cara that it was you. Why would you do that to yourself?

DAVID   I was. I was trying to protect him. Jesus.

DI   It wasn't Nick. It clearly wasn't Jack. But you. You've watched. And you didn't tell me you've watched it.

         You didn't upload it, did you? Please tell me that it wasn't you. I mean you said it before for me to tell Cara like it was a lie but it's not, is it?

DAVID   What? No. No.

DI   Is that the reason you don't want me to call the police? Because he'll find out. You did. Didn't you?

DAVID   It's not what you –

DI   Don't.

DAVID   It's not what you think.

DI   I can't. I can't even.

DAVID   I mean I didn't do it because I was –
         Jesus. Just calm. Just calm

         It was a forum thing.

DI   What?

DAVID   A forum thing. I know it was stupid it was really stupid but –

DI   What do you mean a forum thing –

DAVID   There's this internet forum I go on. Sometimes.
         A Chelsea forum.

DI   Chelsea? Fucking Chelsea?

DAVID   A fans' forum. And they've got this thread. This thread
         where they share where a bunch of the lads –

DI   What lads?

DAVID   The lads on the forum. Where they share you know
         pictures and videos and things mostly random things
         people they don't know people they've found on the
         internet you know girls they like the look of or videos
         that are particularly or are are even funny sometimes
         and they share the links and we comment on them and
         we have a good laugh and when I found it I found that
         video on his computer I don't know. I thought they'd
         like to see it.

         I just. I want you to know. It wasn't a sex thing.
         A wanking thing. I don't. I mean I would never. It was
         a and I know I know this sounds stupid but it was
         more of a dad thing. I was proud of him.

DI   Proud?

DAVID   I don't know do I –

DI   I feel sick.

DAVID   I don't know do I. He's my son and he was. And she's.
         And I just thought. Yeah. You know. Yeah.

         and I put it on the thread and I told them it was my
         boy. And they all. All of them.
         It was stupid I know.
         But I never knew. I never thought that any of this. I'm
         sorry.

         I'm so sorry. I know what you must be thinking.

         It was a dad thing. That was all. A stupid dad thing.

DI   When you were watching it. When you watched them
         have sex, you never thought, you never once thought
         that it looked like –

DAVID   God no. Never.
          Do you think I'd have shared it if I ever thought that?

                              ...

DI

                              ...

DAVID   You're up.

          Did you get any

          Did you sleep at all? I made some coffee. There's
          coffee in the pot.

DI   I'm not going to the police.

DAVID   Right. Okay. That's. That's.

DI   But not for you. Not because of you. You need to
          know that. Because of Jack.
          No, actually. Not because of Jack.
          It's me. I can't do it. I spent all night thinking about it
          and I know that I should do it and I know that he
          deserves it he deserves it more than and I can't stop
          thinking about that girl that girl that he did that to
          But then I thought about actually doing it. About
          actually physically calling the police. And you're
          right. I can't.
          I want all that. I want to see him do his exams and go
          uni and get married and have kids and make a
          difference and not have this this awful this huge thing
          hanging over him for the rest of his life.
          and
          and he did it though. He did it. Sent round the photos
          and made the video and he took that girl
          and he raped her –

DAVID   Don't

DI   What?

DAVID   You don't need to say that word.

DI   And you.
          You put it out there. You put it out there so that
          everyone could see. And we can't let that go. I owe it
          to him not to let that go.

DAVID   We'll talk to him. We'll talk to him. And we'll sort this
          out. Listen.

          About last night. I'm so sorry. You know that I would
          never.

DI   I know what I want to do.

                              ...

DAVID   You can't be serious.

DI   It's the only way

DAVID   It's not the only way.

          There are a billion other ways.

DI   For him. For me actually, as well. Because he is me,
          really, isn't he? He's me and he's you.

DAVID   This isn't how we deal with things.

DI   Why not? My dad did. All the time. Maybe he had it
          right.

DAVID   I don't want to hear about your fucking dad, alright.
          I don't want to hear it.
          We're not like him and we're not like them. We're
          good fucking people. We don't have to resort to to
          What I'm saying is we should handle this. Me and
          you. Not them. No one else.

DI   Me and you?

DAVID   If you do this. If you go through with this that's it. You
          understand. This. Us. That's the end of it. I mean it.

          Don't smile.

DI   I'm not. Believe me.

DAVID   He's a child.

DI   Is he.

DAVID   I'll tell him. I'll tell him that you did this.

DI   You either let me do this or we go to the police. We go to the police and we tell them what's in that video and we tell them who uploaded it. That's the choice.

DAVID   I love you.
Please.
He made a mistake. We both made a mistake. But you don't have to do this. Don't punish Jack because of me. He didn't mean to do anything wrong. Not really.
He's your son.
You don't have to do this.

...

DI   I want to ask you something.

CARA   I'm not gonna help him.

DI   I know.

I'd like to speak to your dad.

CARA   It won't make no difference. Your husband tried already. Dad ripped his shirt.

DI   I heard.

CARA

Cracked me up. He was like 'Please don't Ian, please don't Ian!' He's a bit soft, your husband, in' he?

DI   I've
I've got an offer.
For your dad. And your brother. You too, actually.
I want to offer it to you, too.

CARA   What offer?

DI   When this all started, I thought your dad going after Jack was cos he was stupid. I heard your brother was the same. A thug, that's what I heard.

CARA   People don't know him.

DI   But I realise now that if you were my daughter, my sister, I'd want to kill him too. I don't know if I'd do it. But I'd want to. God I'd want to.

They've got to promise they'll lay off Jack. Stay out of his way. For a month, at least. Enough time so I can bring him home and he can do his exams. You'll tell Jack that you believe he didn't upload the video, you told your family to back off. That if he comes back he'll be safe.

CARA   Why would I do that?

DI   After that, you don't talk to him again. Once his exams are over I'll call you.
        I'll call you and I'll tell you where Jack's gonna be, where he's gonna be alone.

        And then, then
        Then you can have him.
        Your brother, and your dad, they can have him for...
        for twenty minutes. If they want. Twenty minutes alone with him where they do what they need to do, where they do what they need to and I promise you we won't call the police. We won't do anything.

CARA   That's
        Why would you do that?

DI   He's everything to me. You understand?
        All I've ever wanted is to see him have the life he deserves. And if we turn him in, that's gone, that's over. I was going to take him to the police because he deserves it. I decided not to, because I

        But he did what he did to you, and it kills me. It does. So I'm here because he needs to understand
        They both need to understand what he did.

CARA   They?

DI   I'm here, as his mum to ask you and your family to help him learn from it. Learn from it now instead of pay for it later on. Will you do that for me Cara? Will you do it for you?

CARA   What's his dad say about this?

DI   He.

Your brother. Your dad. You too, if you like. And Jack. No one else. Twenty minutes. Twenty minutes where they do what they have to. Where they give him what he needs, within reason.

CARA   Within reason?

DI   I've drawn up a… a list of. Rules. Of things they're not allowed to do.

CARA   You're joking.

DI   I don't want them doing anything too… Nothing permanent.
Nothing he can't get better from. No weapons. No touching the eyes. Or. Or genitals. Nothing like that. Just enough so that he feels. That he knows what he's done.

You understand what I mean Cara? There's a line and if they cross it –

CARA   Yeah. Yeah I get it.

DI   And then I take him, I take him home with me, I take care of him and none of us, not your lot or my lot, none of us talk about this ever again. Jack gets on with his life. You get on with yours. It's finished.
What d'you think?

What d'you think?

CARA   Twenty minutes?

DI   Let me talk to your dad.

CARA   How d'you come up with that number?

DI   I

Why are you laughing?

CARA   I just wondered. You know? What's it about twenty minutes that made you say yeah, yeah that sounds about the right length for what he done. Sounds good to me. I mean fifteen minutes nah that's too short I mean he's practically getting away with it if it's fifteen minutes. But twenty-five minutes would be way too much wouldn't it I mean that would be a bit unfair

on him wouldn't it? Nobody deserves twenty-five
minutes. Not when they've only –
Twenty minutes though yeah yeah

DI   Alright.

CARA   That sounds nice that sounds right yeah bring it on
that's perfect. All sorted. Twenty minutes and then
everything's back to normal. I can go home and you can
take him home and we can all have a nice cup of tea.

DI   Alright. What do you want then?

CARA   What do I want?

DI   How long? How long d'you think –

CARA   Well the video that was only four minutes weren't it so
maybe that's all I deserve?
What's the matter with you? Seriously. I'm actually
asking.
First you come to me screaming at me that I'm lying
begging me to stop Jack getting hurt.

Now you come and you say you believe me and want
my dad and Ian to deal with him like this, you want
them to fuck him up but only if they're really polite
and promise to stick to your really specific guidelines?
You got a screw loose love. Seriously. You're sick in
the head.
What would Jack think about this eh?
Maybe someone should tell him. Maybe someone
should tell him what his mother's really like.

DI   I thought this was
I mean I thought this was what you wanted?

CARA   Yeah, you know what, you're right. All I want is for
him to get slapped around a bit and that'll make me
feel all better. Thank you so much.

DI   But your dad. Your brother. You told them –

CARA   I told them cos they're my dad and my brother. Who
else am I gonna tell? I just wanted someone knowing.
I didn't know what they'd do. But they don't listen.

Course they don't. They went after Jack because they
want an ending to this, just like you. Just like everyone
else. A nice neat end where everyone can thank god
they don't have to think about it any more because
fucking justice was served.
Well fuck them. They'll get bored of him soon
enough. You watch.

DI   So. What then? Tell me what to do.
         I can't get the police involved. I'm sorry but I can't.
         Jack… He needs to know what he did.

CARA   Why?
         So you can go back to your nice house and your nice
         son and sit there feeling like good people because
         what? Because you made him pay? This isn't the way.
         There isn't any way. There ain't no ending. Sorry.

         That video. What he did. That's always there now.
         That's there, that's me for good. Whatever happens to
         me or Jack or you that ain't changing.

         But you want it to be like none of this ever happened?
         Go home and act like none of this ever happened.
         Nothing stopping you. Nothing stopping Jack.

         Twenty minutes? Fuck you.

DI   Don't tell Jack, will you? That I asked you this.

         Please.

CARA   Go home to your son.

                         …

DI   You listening to me?

DAVID   I heard.

DI   You heard what I said?

DAVID   I heard.

DI   Couldn't go through with it. Went to see her I went to
         speak to Cara but before I got there I realised I couldn't
         go through with it, you know, couldn't do that to him.
         I think we should speak to him. I should speak to him.

DAVID   Right.

DI   What's the matter?
What's that face?

DAVID   I just wish you'd said something sooner.

DI   Look at me. Look at me. Oh god.
You didn't tell him, did you? Please tell me you didn't
tell Jack.

DAVID   I.

I'm sorry.

DI   Oh. No. No.

DAVID   I had to.

DI   No no no no no no I didn't go through with it I didn't
fucking go through with it.

DAVID   I didn't know that, did I? I mean Jesus how was
I supposed to know.
The very idea that you'd get so close that you'd even
consider

DI   How much did you tell him?

DAVID   It's disgusting. He's your son.

DI   Disgusting?

DAVID   I told him everything. I had to. Didn't want him
getting hurt.

DI   What did. What did he say?

DAVID   What d'you think? He's devastated.

DI   Should never have said anything to you.

DAVID   I warned you that I would. But you didn't listen. You
never do.

DI   I need to see him. Talk to him. Explain.

DAVID   He's gone.

DI   Gone where?

DAVID   I don't think I should tell you. He asked me not to tell you. At least for a while.

DI   Oh.

Okay.

DAVID   I'm sorry. But come on. What else did you expect? I'm his dad.

DI   I'll tell him. I'll tell him you uploaded the video.

DAVID   Come on.

DI   Tell him how 'proud' you were of him. How you just had to share it.

DAVID   What good will that do?

DI   Show him what his father's really like.

DAVID   So what? So you can score some points back? Is that what this is about? I was trying to keep him safe. I was thinking about Jack's welfare. All you're doing is being petty.

DI   Petty? You told him. Before I'd even done anything you fucking told him.

DAVID   I didn't actually.

DI   What?

DAVID   I didn't tell him. I haven't spoken to him. Not yet anyway.

DI   Why. Why would you

DAVID   Well, now you know don't you? You know what it would feel like if he did know.

DI   Jesus Christ.

DAVID   If I did tell him.

DI   Who the fuck are you?

DAVID   I'm just looking out for my son.

DI   Our son.

DAVID   I don't want him facing any more disruptions. Not now.

        That video. I don't think there's any point in telling
        him how it got uploaded, do you? It
        would crush him.

        Just like, and I'm not being funny, but you see now
        how much it would crush him if he found out his own
        mum had wanted him hurt. If I was forced to tell him
        the truth. You get what I'm saying?

DI   I used. Used to be able to tell when you were lying.

DAVID   Jack doesn't find out about any of this. Understand?
        We get him home and he carries on as normal.

DI   Normal.

DAVID   Listen. Love. I'm sorry I had to do that.
        But I'm so glad, so glad you changed your mind, that
        you didn't go through with it, because that would have
        been the end for us. And I don't want that. Neither of
        us want that.

        This way, at least, we can still be a team. Me and you,
        eh?

DI   Me and you.

        I didn't change my mind.

        It wasn't that I changed my mind. She turned me down.

        She turned me down, and if she hadn't I would've
        gone through with it in a heartbeat. I would have
        handed your son over and I wouldn't have blinked.

                              ...

NICK   Can I help you with something?

        Hello-o?
        Can. I. Help. You. With. Something?
        Oh it's you. Sorry.

DI   Nick. Hello.
        Didn't recognise you.

NICK   S'okay. Didn't mean to be rude about you standing there. You know, if I'd known it was you rather than a normal customer I'd've been bit more polite.

DI   You work here now then?

NICK   How'd you guess?

DI   Not seen you... how are things?

NICK   Yeah yeah you know. Work here. Still here. That's it really.
How's Jack getting on?

DI   He.

NICK   He's at Durham, innit?

DI   That's right.

NICK   Seen some photos he put up. You seen them?

DI   No.

NICK   Looks a good laugh.
I'd show you but. No phones while I'm on shift.
What's he doing again?

DI   Law.

NICK   Law. That's right. Shit.
Not spoken to him in a while. Not since results.

I better

DI   Good seeing you.

NICK   He smashed it, didn't he?
He did well, I mean. His results. He was always gonna do well.

DI   Yeah.
Yeah he did well.

NICK   You tell him I said hello?

DI   He did really well.

ROSS & RACHEL

For Dad, who was nothing like this

Acknowledgements

Thuli and Em, who helped us find out what the hell this was.

Emily, who has been very patient.

And Andrew and Tom, who have helped build this thing from the ground up. This play is as much by them as it is me.

J.F.

Ross & Rachel was first produced by MOTOR and performed in The Box at the Assembly George Square Theatre, as part of the Edinburgh Festival Fringe 2015, on 6 August 2015. The show then transferred to the 2016 Brits Off Broadway Festival at 59e59 Theaters in New York, and Battersea Arts Centre in London, before embarking on a UK tour. The cast was as follows:

Molly Vevers

Director	Thomas Martin
Designer	Alison Neighbour
Production Manager	Nick Slater
Lighting Designer	Douglas Green
Sound Designer	Jon McLeod
Producer	Andrew Hughes (MOTOR)
Production Manager	Simeon Miller
(for original Edinburgh run)	
Sound Associate	Bethany Taylor
(for original Edinburgh run)	
Production Assistant	Andrey Khrzhanovskiy
(for original Edinburgh run)	

Note

This is a play with two voices for one performer.

The performer should use their own accent.

Sometimes, I just get really fucking sick of it. Don't you?

No.

Never?
No.
I've always loved it I don't know why you'd
It's nothing to do with you it's just
What?
Don't worry about it.
What?
Don't give me that look I said don't worry about it.
I'm not looking like anything.
It's nothing to do with us I just don't like people thinking we
come as a package.
We do come as a package.
Like we're the same person or
We're a team
Right but
They see us as a team. That's a good thing.
Right, I know but.
I see us as a team don't you see us as a team?
Right yeah of course but when somebody emails you something
that's meant for both of us, I don't see why they can't just email
me as well.
It's just easier that way.
But it's always you. They always email you, but address it to the
both of us.
You're worried about emails?
Forget it.
No go on.
It's fine.
I want to understand.
It's just. I don't know when people started saying our names
together. You know? I don't know when that happened.
We are together.
Yes, but, I mean. Why do they always have to say my name
second?

Happy birthday to you happy birthday to

Thank you

Thank you

Thank you for coming

We're so pleased you could make it.

Forty-five. I know, I know.

You don't look it. Tell her she doesn't look it.

Stop it. You're embarrassing them.

Hey so glad to see you.

You guys make the cutest couple we were just saying weren't we honey?

We were, yeah.

How long have you two been together now? You've still got that look about you.

Did you ever hear how we first met? Right from the first moment I saw her, standing next to my sister, I knew.

Not now, honey.

Strap yourselves in, you're not gonna believe this story.

They don't want to hear about that.

You guys think that's good? Tell them about how we got back together. She tells it better than I can.

No, I don't.

Of course you do!

Let's just enjoy

Tell them! Isn't that the most romantic story?

She's perfect. She's a prom queen and I'm a nerd.

Honey

She's a prom queen and she belongs to me. Doesn't that make you feel great about the world?

Let's talk about something else.

Tell them about the time we

Not. Now.

Tell them.

Tell them.

Tell them!

Right from the first moment I saw her, standing next to my sister, I knew.

Don't look at me like that.

I would never cheat on him.

It's not anything serious, Daniel's just a friend from work that's all.

Okay, so we held hands in the office kitchen. Briefly. But it wasn't even a

I am so lucky to have her. When she walks through the door every evening I still get that feeling you know? Just like. Wow. She's mine, you know?
That woman belongs to me and I can't believe my luck.

But I've been staying at work longer and longer and then I come home to.
I come home to him and it's just. You know. It's not *bad* but.

I can't do it. I can't have this argument again.
It's not an argument it's a discussion.
It's my job. What do you want me to do?
Leave on time. I manage it.
Your job is different to mine.
Less important?
Nothing's changed.
What do you mean?
This is the same argument we were having in our twenties and you remember how that turned out.
Oh I wondered when you were going to bring that up. We were on a –
Don't say it. Do not say it. If you say that word I swear I will walk out that door.
I wasn't going to. Look at me. I wasn't. Listen, I'm sorry, I just want to spend some time together that's all.

True love.
That's what our relationship is.

It's not that I regret it, exactly.

People always say that without really meaning it don't they.
But that's what it is.

I mean we were on again off again on again off again for so long.
Well you know. You were there.

It's like, I have to know what she's doing, all the time, just so I can picture her doing it, I can feel close to her or. I'll be like, 'Hey, what are you doing?' and she'll text back like, 'I'm at work' or 'I'm at lunch with so-and-so' and then I'm like 'Okay!' and I just feel better.

Sometimes I'll just show up at her work and take her to lunch.
Just surprise her, you know?

I feel guilty talking to you like this. Things aren't so bad really.

So where shall we go?
I don't know honey. Somewhere close by. I'm very busy.
I know this new place that you're gonna love.
Is it a long walk? It's just I've got to get back to the office.
Wait.
Honey? Did you hear me? Is it a long walk because I promised
Bill that I'd.
Wait. I feel. F F
What?
F-for
What's the matter?
F-for for for f f
Oh my god. What's wrong? Honey? Your face it's all
For out out out t t t
Oh my god.
T t t t t t
Oh my god help us please please somebody help him somebody
help him!

We're getting married!

What time is it?

We're getting married!

God damn my neck is sore. There's a stain on the hospital
curtains.

*We're getting married again in the place where we had our
first date because an unexpected catastrophe struck our original
venue.*
All our friends from down the years are in attendance.

Don't wake him up.

*My best friend is the best man and my other best friend is
conducting the ceremony.*

Which way is the bathroom? Thank you.
God. I look awful.

*I'm nervous because a series of unlikely events has delayed
the bride's arrival and I'm starting to worry she's not going
to show.*

He's tossing and turning.
Always sleeps funny in a strange bed.
Jesus. It's so fucking hot in here.

*The music starts, and comically mismatched pairs of my family
and friends walk down the aisle.
Everything is perfectly positioned.*

Really need to get some sleep.

*The music changes and there's a gasp as she walks in looking
more beautiful than I have ever seen her.
As she reaches me, I tell her she is my Princess Leia.
Everybody awws.*

*There is a mix-up with the vows. Everybody laughs.
And then it's done. And then we kiss and we kiss and cheering
cheering from the audience.*

*Everybody is so happy for us and they turn to each other and
they say thank god they finally did it. We've been waiting for this
wedding for years. The whole world has been waiting for this
wedding for years.*

*She tosses the bouquet and the bridesmaids all tackle each other
and then the crowd parts and somebody unexpected is holding it
and it's the funniest thing we've ever seen.*

*Our first dance in the place where we had our first date, and the
stars are shining above us, and our beautiful children are there,
my daughter is so tall and my son is with his girlfriend and we're
married again and suddenly we're on the stairs of the* Titanic *and
we're kissing and all our old friends from the boat are bursting
into applause and then*

Where am I?

Are you okay honey?
Didn't mean to wake you.

I can feel it in my brain. It itches.

Ten minutes until our meeting with the consultant.
He'll tell me that the tumour in my brain is benign. Right?
That's what he's going to tell me.
Of course that's what he's going to tell me.

That elevator came a bit quickly didn't it and that doctor's door
was closer to the elevator than I would have liked and oh look
he's opened the door almost instantly and oh great we're inside.

No. Put it out of your head.
I didn't have to be in this room.
Not now.
The two chairs in the doctor's office are different colours.
Keep a straight face. I want her to think that I'm calm.
He looks terrified.

The doctor is still talking.
Oh fuck oh fuck oh positives oh fuck oh treatable oh fuck oh
fuck oh plan of action.

I'm not going anywhere.
I'm not going anywhere.
I'm not going anywhere.

Just another morning. Just another morning.
Where's my dinosaur tie? You seen my dinosaur tie?
Have a nice day.
You too. Don't overdo it.
Don't worry. I've given this lecture a hundred times before.

Five minutes until lunch with Daniel. Maybe we'll go to that
Vietnamese place round the corner and I'll tell him what's going
on, and he'll hold my hand and he'll say oh no I'm so sorry are
you okay and then he'll say do you want to go for a walk and
he'll put his arm around me and he'll say it's going to be alright.
And maybe I'll look up at him and then we'll stop and then he'll
kiss me. And at first it's really tentative and then we just sorta
sink into it and at first his hands start on my waist and then they
come up and they're in my hair and
Sorry say that again I was miles away.

Maybe I should tell my students what I'm fighting. I'll make a
joke about it so that they'll all be impressed by my strength in the
face of adversity and they can smile at me in the corridor and say

how are you doing how are you feeling oh I'm so sorry to hear oh
Professor I was thinking of running a half-marathon in your
honour I was thinking of growing a moustache for your cancer.

Daniel seems genuinely worried about me.
Thank you.
That hug lasted just a second too long.
Didn't it?
I'm sorry Daniel, I need to take this.

My phone has been going off all day. You told everyone?!
I thought they'd want to know.
On the fucking internet?
What's wrong with that?
Without even talking to me? And oh, surprise surprise, you've
signed it from both of us.
I couldn't have just put my name. It would have looked weird.
Read it. I said some really nice things about you.

Look at me. Hey. Look at me. I know you're worried. I'll be fine.
Trust me. This isn't how this ends.

He's very strong.
She's my rock.
How you feeling?
CAT scan on Wednesday.
She's been great, you know.
We're just taking each day
We're getting through it you know
We're
We're
We're
Diet plan.
Medication charts.
How you feeling?
The consultant.
Pills.
Chemo.
Frontal lobe.
Radio.
Coffee?
He'd love to see you.
Swelling.

Steroids.
Thank you for the flowers.
I'm going to be sick.
Coffee?
Side effects.
Oh.
Coffee?
Juice?
Cream?
What time's the appointment?
D'you take sugar?
Oh.
So great to see you.
Thought they'd never leave.
Beer?
Coffee? Coffee? Coffee? Coffee? Coffee? Coffee? Coffee?
Coffee? Coffee? Coffee? Coffee? Coffee? Coffee? Coffee?
Coffee? Coffee? Coffee? Coffee? Coffee? Coffee? Coffee?
Coffee? Coffee? Coffee? Coffee? Coffee? Coffee? Coffee?
Coffee? Coffee? Coffee? Coffee? Coffee? Coffee? Coffee?
Coffee? Coffee? Coffee? Coffee? Coffee? Coffee? Coffee?
Coffee? Coffee? Coffee? Can I get you a coffee? Coffee? Coffee?
Coffee? Coffee? Coffee? Coffee? Coffee? Coffee? Coffee?
Coffee? Coffee? Coffee? Coffee? Coffee? Coffee? Coffee?
Coffee? Coffee? Coffee? Coffee? Coffee? Coffee? Coffee?
Coffee? Coffee? Coffee? Coffee? Coffee? Coffee? Coffee?
Coffee? Coffee? Coffee? Coffee? Coffee? Coffee? Coffee?
Coffee? Coffee? Coffee? Coffee? Coffee? Coffee? Coffee?
Coffee? Coffee? Coffee? Coffee? Coffee? Coffee? Coffee?
Coffee? Coffee? Coffee? Coffee? Coffee? Coffee? Coffee?
Coffee? Coffee? Coffee? Coffee?

Wait.
What.

Oh.

Up to a year.

I've
Got.
He.
Has.

Anywhere up to
Anywhere up to a year.
Are you okay?
I'm fine.
I'm fine.
I don't think he's fine.
I'm fine.
A year's a long time.
A year's a long time.
This is our end and it's.
It hits you like a bullet news like that. It hits you like a train and
I'm devastated that –
But actually. No.
You know what?
If I'm honest.
If I'm totally honest I feel. Deep down.
And this is just between us right?
I. Feel.
Because the thing about him, the thing that I forgot all those
years that we were broke up in our twenties and thirties. The
thing about him is he's actually really. Fucking. Boring. We have
nothing in common, is that horrible to say? I'm not sure we ever
did. Sometimes he talks to me and you know what?
I couldn't give less of a shit. No. No I don't mean that. Please
don't tell anyone I said that. I'm just. I'm just tired is all.

The thing about her is

He doesn't care about my work, about anything I'm interested in,
I just happened to be the first woman he got to know that wasn't
his fucking mom and then bam, here we are. He had
a crush on his sister's best friend and then somehow we both
ended up here, and I'm going through this and it's driving me
crazy it's driving me fucking crazy because this is not what
I had in mind for my forties let me tell you. I'm sorry I shouldn't
be saying this to you I'm just tired I'm just really fucking tired.

She's mine. And I know that won't change. Even when I'm.
Right from the first moment I saw her, standing next to my sister,
I knew. She belonged to me.

When we first got back together I thought it was just a part of
getting used to each other again. But that feeling never went

away and now I've been on the brink of leaving for. But I don't.
I haven't left.
Because.
Because well, you know. It's me and him.

This is really boring.

.

I want to strike up a friendship with a sassy nurse who says
something sassy at precisely the right moment to break the tension.

I want there to be mishap with my hospital gown that leaves me
stranded naked in the corridor having to use a fire extinguisher to
cover my genitals.
I want to look in the bed next to me and oh my god it's my high-
school football coach who yells my last name and says get down
and give me twenty.
I want her to put down her magazine and to take my hand and
give me the speech that I hope she's going to give me where she
tells me that she loves me and that we make the perfect team and
we'll face this together and that our strength as a couple is more
than a match for what's going on inside my body.
Wouldn't everybody love that?
I can't stop
Can't stop worrying about what she'll do when I'm gone.
This can't actually be the end for us. Can it?
You okay honey?
I'm fine.

Daniel! Oh my god.
That's hilarious.
Me, go to Australia, with him?
It's just a joke.
I can feel myself.
Just a joke.

Listen, I, and I don't know how to say this Daniel, it's a bit
awkward really but I don't think we should spend time like this.
Any more. And I know, I know we're just friends and it's not that
I don't enjoy it but what with everything at home…
Oh. He gets it. He's not fighting me.
Thanks for being such a great friend, I knew you'd understand.

Look at all those couples.
Look at all those fucking couples out there.
Which one will leave. Which one will run. Which one is cheating
on the other. Which one will die first. Him. Him.
Her. Him.
Look at that girl there. She's what? Mid-twenties? Look at how
she looks at him.
I was just her. Wasn't I? And now. How did that happen? I was
just her.
She has no fucking idea what's coming for her. None of them do.

Grab her. Tell her it's not going to turn out like that you young
fucking stupid fucking idiot it doesn't work that way. It's not
about hand-holding. It's not about first dates. It's not about will
they won't they or on again off again or he's the one or weddings
or new-baby smell or airport reconciliations and the people who
tell you it is are liars they are liars and they'll keep telling you it's
about all that but it's not. It's about everything in between.
Off she goes. Happy as a fucking songbird.

How are you feeling, honey?
Fine.
The least he deserves. To be there for him. That's what I'm for,
right? That's what I'm for.
Because he does love me. And I.
I said that I'd be there for him.
Fuck.
Did he just feel me recoil?

I can feel it
I can feel it inside my head it feels itchy feels like a scab like
a spider bite right here and so I reach into my pocket and I take
out my keys and I find the pointy one that opens our front door
and I stand in front of the mirror and I take a deep breath and
I open my eyes wide wide like this and I hold them open and
I take the point the point of the key and I go in behind the eye
through the side and it goes black and I start to dig, dig behind
the eye and I feel the squish and then I hit bone I hit bone at the
back of the socket. I keep gouging and I scratch scratch scratch
until I've made a hole in the bone and then I'm in and I can feel
it and I dig so hard and I get right in there and I scrape it out
I scrape it out of my head and I hold it in my hand a black lump
black dirty gristle and then I flush it I flush it and then

She's still asleep.
The keys on the bedside table.
Try to fall back to sleep.

Hi Daniel.
No, I
He's trying. At least he's still trying.
I can't I'm
Not tonight, maybe
All I want to say is

He's stopped trying.
He's not Daniel any more. He's just Daniel from work. Daniel
across the hall. Daniel who's dating Julie or Jessica. Daniel who's
moving back to Australia?
Oh. Great. That's exciting.
Home. Hiya. How you feeling?
Anywhere up to a year.
Up to a year.

He's coming up from LA.
Really? Why?
He wants to see you.
He looks fat.
You boys have fun. Don't let him drink too much.

TWO MORE PLEASE. BOURBON. I DON'T KNOW, WHAT
DO YOU HAVE? YEAH. YEAH THAT SOUNDS GOOD. IS
THAT GOOD?

THE BARMAN LOOKS LIKE A GOOD GUY. I WAS JUST
TELLING MY FRIEND, YOU LOOK LIKE A GOOD GUY!
AND HOW ARE YOU, BY THE WAY? THAT'S GOOD.
THAT'S GOOD. LONG SHIFT? ARE YOU WORKING A
LONG SHIFT?
LISTEN. WANNA KNOW SOMETHING? I HAVE CANCER.
NO NO, HE DOESN'T MIND, DO YOU? YOU DON'T MIND.
YOU CAN ASK MY DOCTOR YOU DON'T BELIEVE ME.
NO, NO, THAT'S NICE OF YOU TO SAY, THANK YOU.
THESE THINGS HAPPEN, YOU KNOW? THAT'S NICE.
THAT'S NICE OF YOU. HOW OLD ARE YOU MAN?
TWENTY? TWENTY-ONE?
I WAS TOP OF MY CLASS, DO YOU KNOW THAT? PHD.
I'M A *DOC-TOR*. NOT THAT THAT.
I'M GOING TO BE A HUGE LOSS TO MY FIELD. THEY'LL
WRITE THINGS ABOUT ME, YOU KNOW?

LISTEN TO ME. MY WIFE? SHE'S. SHE'S. SHE'S FUCKIN'
BEAUTIFUL, MAN. SHE IS. DO YOU WANT TO SEE? LET
ME. HERE. I'VE GOT A PHOTO. SHE'S. VERY.
SUPPORTIVE. SHE IS. I AM SO LUCKY TO HAVE HER.
BUT. NO.
HERE. LOOK AT THIS
ACTUALLY NO, NO WAIT. I HAVE A YOUNGER PHOTO.

HOLD ON.

HOLD ON!

HERE'S WHAT SHE LOOKED LIKE WHEN WE FIRST GOT
TOGETHER. SHE'S TWENTY-FIVE IN THAT PICTURE.

RIGHT? FUCKING SUPERMODEL RIGHT?

HE KNOWS. YOU TOTALLY WOULD, *RIGHT*? IF YOU SAW
THAT WALKING ROUND CAMPUS, YOU'D BE

NO, NO COME ON WE'RE JUST HAVING A
CONVERSATION.

BUT SHE KNOWS. SHE KNOWS WHAT SHE'S LOSING.
SHE WON THE FUCKING LOTTERY GETTING WITH ME,
YOU KNOW? BECAUSE SHE MIGHT BE BEAUTIFUL. SHE
MIGHT HAVE RICH FUCKING PARENTS BUT I'M A
FUCKING SMART

MAN. I'M A SMART, WHITE, SMART FUCKING MAN WHO
KNOWS HOW TO TAKE CARE OF HER, AND WHO LOVES
HER, AND I'VE FUCKING GOT MY SHIT TOGETHER,
AND, YOU KNOW, AND THAT'S, THAT'S THE FUCKIN'
GOLDEN TICKET WHEN IT COMES TO

TO

GOOD LUCK TRYIN' TO FIND ANOTHER ONE OF ME,
THAT'S WHAT I'M SAYING.

I FUCKIN' LOVE HER THOUGH. I DO. I DO. SHE WAS. WE
KNEW EACH OTHER AS TEENAGERS, DID YOU KNOW
THAT? SHE'S A PROM QUEEN AND SHE BELONGS TO
ME. DOESN'T THAT MAKE YOU FEEL FUCKING

AND I CAN'T STOP PICTURING HER ALL ALONE
WITHOUT ME AND THAT MAKES ME SADDER THAN
ANYTHING.

WE GOT A KID, YOU KNOW THAT? WE GOT A
BEAUTIFUL LITTLE GIRL. SHE LOOKS JUST LIKE HER
MOM, SHE DOES. SHE'S GOT HER LOOKS AND MY
BRAINS. SHE'S GONNA BE SO BEAUTIFUL WHEN SHE
HOW OLD ARE YOU? TWENTY? TWENTY-ONE?

HEY!

TAXI! HEY!

AH. FUCK.

TAXI!!

Bed. Don't wake her up.

Don't. Wake. Her…

*I'm alone on the rooftop of the apartment I had when I was a
young woman and the sky full of stars is so bright that it hurts my
eyes to look at. I turn and I feel my hand being taken and I'm
whirled around the dance floor and when I look up I realise that
what I'm dancing with is a six-foot lobster. The lobster spins me
around and it won't let go and I see that the stars are not the
stars but actually the lights of the ceiling a projection and we're
lying on a picnic blanket and we're wet we're soaked through
actually because I just rolled over the juice box. The lobster gets
up and beckons only now I can't see his face, and every time I try
and get around to his front he gets a little further away until he is
outside in the rain oh god he's outside and I'm trapped behind a
glass door a glass door to a coffee shop that has been bolted
several times and it's raining and he bangs his head upon the
windowpane and he wants to come in, he wants to come in, he*

I can feel it more and more.
Headaches and nausea and
And we're
I can taste metal in my mouth.
I'm so tired but I can't say anything.
His sense of smell is not
What will it be like?
What will it actually be like when it happens?
I want to ask but I don't ask.
Honey?
What is it actually going to feel like.
Honey are you?
I want to know. I want to know. I don't want to know. I want
to know.
Do I feel myself soften or
Honey are you feeling okay?
Will she tell me, will she tell me when I've got a week left?
A day left? An hour?
And what happens after?
What happens after it's done?

I have a picture of my life after he's gone.
I'll still live in our house.
I'll still see our friends.
I'll still raise our daughter.

And every day little things remind me that he used to be here and now he's not.

Everything feels

For the first few months I can't move for visitors. They all want to take me out for coffee.

And then that stops. They go back to their lives.

I'm left all alone and

And you know what.

I'm okay.

It's actually really great.

I miss him sometimes

But

It's horrible but I'm excited I'm actually a bit excited to find out who I am when he's not around any more.

To live without an 'and' in front of my name.

I start making selfish decisions.

I start putting my job first again. And it works.

I become more successful than I could ever have imagined.

Because I love my job.

I've always loved my job.

And I'm good at it. I'm so fucking good at it. I have the time to start my own business and it actually goes really well.

My daughter and I become closer than ever. She grows into a better woman than I could have hoped.

I have dates and flings and they're fun and strange and not quite But mostly, it's just me. And that's not because of anyone else, it's not because of what our friends might say, it's not because of loyalty.

It's because that's what I want.

And then, at some point, that changes. Maybe when my daughter has gone off to college. Maybe before then.

I meet a kind, handsome man. Not Daniel from work. Maybe Daniel from work.

I feel like I'm going to vomit. Oh.

It's strange to be with someone new but it's also exciting and he talks to me in a way that I'd forgotten was even possible.

Eventually we move in together and when he proposes he does it somewhere hot. Maybe we have a small wedding in the spring and after the honeymoon we move to Paris where I've always dreamed of working.

Whatever happens after you're gone, I promise I'll be happy.
Why did I just tell him that?
Why did she just tell me that?
Maybe I think it will make him feel better.
Maybe I think it will make him feel worse.

I want her to be happy. I want her to find somebody else.
And I know she will. Because she's still a young woman a
beautiful woman and that's how things go, isn't it?
She'll find someone else straight away and she'll spend many
years with him, maybe even more years than she spent with me.
And that's okay.
I know that maybe when she dies aged eighty it will be him that
talks at her funeral and I'll be referred to as her *first* husband.
And that's okay. That's fine. It will be him and not me who sees
our children, my children, who gets to know the people they
become. It will be him who holds my grandchild. Him who's
buried next to her.
Him who gets to be with her who gets to eat with her and walk
with her and sleep with her and kiss her and fuck her and and
hear her laugh and see her get old while I'm. I'm. What?
Nothing. Nowhere.
It will be him who becomes the love of her life and that is.
That is
That's absolutely fine.
Of course I want her to find someone else. She deserves it.
Of course.
Although.
Fuck her and whoever she finds. It's not right, it's not right, you
know, because this is, this is me and her. I hope she feels guilty.
I hope the guilt it chokes her. I hope whoever he is he treats her
like shit. I hope he beats her. I hope he treats her well. I hope he
cheats on her. I hope she's happy. I hope she's unhappy. I love
her so much.

Honey, are you okay?

I can picture it. Her and him her new husband and his hands his
hands all over her I want to be sick I want to be sick get off her
you asshole you fucking asshole she belongs to me she belongs
to me. She belongs. To. Me.
No. No. This can't be it, this isn't what was supposed to happen.
This is not the end of me and her.

He's hanging on in there. We're doing fine thanks for asking. He's strong, so strong, you know? Except he's not strong. He's boring.

But actually. Look at her.
Maybe it's okay. Maybe she's worried about the same thing. How can she go on without me?
That's what she's thinking.
How can she go on without me?

I've got to get out of this house. I love him. We've got nothing to say to each other. I can't remember the last time I talked about television or politics or gossip or anything that wasn't to do with –

Now that's an idea.
A way for this to end where
God, wouldn't that be –
Jesus Christ what's the matter with me.
Think about something else.

It's like he's given up.
No, Mom, he just sits there. He won't do anything. No I've tried. I've tried talking to him, but you know what he's like.

Can't help coming back to the same idea.
Would she consider it? I could ask her.
Maybe…
Come on. Stop it. Get a fucking grip.

Come on honey.
Let's turn the TV off. Yeah? It's a beautiful day.
Let's take a walk.
Let's go for dinner.
Let's go for coffee.
Let's go and see your parents.
Let's go to the park.
Let's go to the movies.
Let's take a holiday.
Let's stay on a yacht.
Let's take a cruise.
Let's see the world.
Let's swim with dolphins.
Let's swim with some fucking dolphins! How about we just take you out there and let's get you kitted up and let's throw you in the sea with some smart fucking dolphins and you can swim until

your legs hurt and your eyes sting and the dolphins have bruised
you from nuzzling too hard and you're tired and the dolphins are
tired and let's get a photo of you in the water with your thumb up
honey, let's get a photo of the dolphin smiling next to you and we
can share it we can send it to your mum and dad we can send it to
all our friends and we can keep that, me and the kids we can keep
that for ever.
Let's do a bungee jump.
Let's do a fucking bungee jump, how about that? Honey, eh?
How about we do. That.
Let's turn the TV off. Yeah?
Let's take a walk.
Okay. What are we watching?

Can't stop thinking about it.
I wonder. I couldn't ask her. I could never ask her. Could I? But
maybe. Maybe
What better way to end things?

Thank you so much for stopping by. He's not at his best
today but.
How are the twins?
Coffee? Beer?
Come in. Sit down. We're watching TV.

It's not like it hasn't happened before.
The Japanese even have a word for it.

Thank you so much for coming.
Some days are better than others. He gets confused.

I know what her answer will be. I know what her answer will be
and I'm terrified but I'm excited.
Everyone has always hated seeing her with someone else.
Everyone hates it when she's alone.
They'll understand.
They know what this relationship means. To us. To everyone.
I'll talk to her tonight.

He looks tired. His face looks odd. I'll have another glass
of wine.
Take her hand.
He's taken my hand.
Do you love me?

Do I love him?
Of course.
Of course, she says!
Something's not right.
Completely?
Of course, what's up? Don't blink.
You do. I know you do.
He's shaking.
Is everything alright? Do you need me to call someone?
When the time comes
Oh god.
When I get too ill, I've decided that I want to finish things
myself.
This isn't a surprise.
Okay. Okay. If you want to, if that's really what you want,
we can talk about it. We can talk about how.
He's smiling.

I've been thinking and, and I really think that this could be, could
be a really beautiful thing. I've been thinking what if, what if,
what if you did it too?
What if I did what too honey?
That smile.
Wait.
He can't mean
He doesn't mean?
I want you to do it too.
I
I want us to do it
Together.
What do you think?
I I
It's what everyone wants.

She looks me in the eye and she says
She says yeah. I will do that with you.
Of course I will because we're one really, aren't we?
She's just a girl, standing in front of a boy. She completes me. To
me, she is perfect.
And now I can't believe this is happening. I can't believe that this
is what we're going to do. They'll think we're mad. They will
write that it's a terrible tragedy for two young parents to take

their life. They will write that it's a terrible tragedy for a beautiful young woman like her to take her life.

But it's not a terrible tragedy. This is the perfect end to our story. And that's been obvious right from the start.

We sit down at the kitchen table to talk through the specifics. She takes my hand in hers and says to me honey, this is all I've ever wanted. You and me. Together for ever.

We talk about when and we talk about where. We talk about who we're going to tell and how we're going to say goodbye. We talk about what music we will play and what clothes we will wear. We talk about the lighting.

We're getting everything in order as if we were planning a wedding. We've told my sister, and she is being very supportive. She has even made a to-do list because that's what my sister does.

I'm excited but I'm terrified but I'm excited.

We write out a note to the kids and a second note to our friends that is full of references to jokes we made in our youth.

Everybody laughs a sad laugh. Hand in hand we go upstairs and we prepare to run our bath. The one with the perfect ending.

She is looking into my eyes as the bath begins to fill.

We say

We say the things that we were always meant to say.

We fill it right to the brim. Not so it spills.

And then, before she gets in we kiss. We kiss a kiss that has the audience on their feet.

It's always been you.

As she lowers herself into the bath she looks more beautiful than ever. I say she is my Princess Leia. Everybody laughs. Everybody sighs.

I pass her the razor and she smiles a sad smile a happy smile. I show her where to make the incision. Right here. The music starts. A short gasp and then

As the water turns red in slow motion I hold her hand. I hold her hand. It's okay, I say. It's okay. It's okay.

And then it's my turn and I hold the razor and I count to three and

The perfect ending. Everyone is waiting to applaud.

One.

Two.

What if I did what too honey?
That smile.
Wait.
He can't mean
He doesn't mean?
I want you to do it too.
I
I want us to do it
Together.
What do you think?
I I
It's what everyone wants.

He's joking. Of course he's joking.
He hasn't made a joke in months but still, he must be joking.
But.
His eyes. His mouth.
He isn't.
Oh god, he isn't joking.

Calm down, honey, you're confused.
You're not thinking straight.
That's far too tight.

Look him in the eye.
Look him in the eye and say
No.
No!
Of course not. Of course I can't do that. Won't do that. Ever. Ever
ever ever.
That's just
Mad.
Fucking madness.

To think of me
To be so
And your children your fucking children.
Get off me.
Please.
Ow that hurts that fucking hurts.
Please.
Get off me.
Please!

GET OFF!
Thank god.
I didn't know what he was going to do. I didn't know what he
was going to do.

Hello? Yes he's had, had some sort of turn or. Well I don't know,
he won't stop, won't stop sobbing. He grabbed me and. Please
come quickly.
Look at him.
I can't be here.
To ask me that.
I'll wait for the ambulance to come and I'll tell them what
happened and while they are talking to him I'll walk out
that door.
I'll go to my mom's house. God.
What am I going to tell her.

I can't sit still.
I feel terrible.
I feel sick.
And meanwhile he is
He is
For the first time since I can remember I don't know how
he's doing.
What's the matter with me?
I shouldn't have left him like that.

I am still so angry with him.
But his room is horrible.
The view from his window is of a wall.
And he looks.
His face looks.

Do you want me to change the channel? Did you hear me honey?
Do you want me to change the channel?
You can go in.
He's on a lot of morphine so he might not
Honey? Look who's come to see you.

I won't tell anyone what he asked me. I don't think I ever will.

Hi Mom.
No, no he's not in any pain because of the
God I'm tired. I'm so fucking tired.

The things he did to me when we were young the time he spied
on me the time he wrote those things or his constant jealousy or
the time he cheated on me with that girl from the that girl from
the why now why am I thinking about that now it's been years.
Stop it stop it stop it.
What's the matter with me? Try and focus on the good things.
How he kissed me when.
It's my birthday and, and he's bought me
The girl the girl from the what's the matter with me the girl the
girl the fights what's the matter with me what he asked me every
last cruel word he ever said to me stop it stop it.
He hasn't woken at all this morning.
Coffee?

The doctor says he can still hear me.
Should say something to him before
A speech, or
I can't. Or. I don't want to.
I really don't want to.

What's the time?
His face.
I think. I think his breathing's changed.

Honey? Can you hear me?

*As she lowers herself into the bath she looks more beautiful than
ever. I say she is my Princess Leia. Everybody laughs. Everybody
sighs.*
I pass her the razor and she smiles a sad smile a happy smile.

I show her where to make the incision. Right here. The music
starts. A short gasp and then
As the water turns red in slow motion I hold her hand. I hold her
hand. It's okay, I say. It's okay. It's okay.
And then it's my turn and I hold the razor and I count to
three and
The perfect ending. Everyone is waiting to applaud.
One.
Two.

My eyes.

The bath?
Where where am I oh no oh no.

Shh.

She's still here she's still here where am I?

Shh. It's okay. I'm here. His eyes.

No I don't want this. I don't want this.

It's okay honey. His eyes are open. Should his

I can hear you.

I'm just going to. I'll be back in a minute honey I'm just going to
go get someone.

Where did you go? Fuck you where did you go you fucking bitch
come back come back.

This is it.
I think this might be it.
In a moment it will just be

me.
His eyes are open, he's very restless, is there anything you can
give him?

Please.
I'm thirsty. Who. I can see.

What do you want? What can I get you? I don't know what
he wants.

Please.
Don't stay.

Can't you give him something?
Thank you. His breathing.

My eyes.
Get off.
Hold me.
Where am I.
What hurts.
My eyes.
Don't stay.
I'm thirsty.
Who said.
What time.
Who said that.

It's okay. It's just me here. Me and you.

My throat.
I don't.
Her face.
My house.
What time.
I'm thirsty.
How old.
Why this.
Air.
What's that.
Where are.

It's okay. I'm here.

Don't let me.
Water.
Hello.
Help.
Where is she.
Don't let me.
No one told me.
What is.
Where is.
Water. Water.

My mouth.
I am.
What's happening.
What's.
No one told me.
No one told me.
No one told me.
No no no
No no.

Please.

I'm thirsty.
I'm.

I think that's it.

It's just me.

Oh.

I'm the only one here.

twins

twins was first performed as part of The Miniaturists, at the Arcola Theatre, London, on 15 November 2015. The cast was as follows:

THE TWINS   Simona Bitmate
                                    Phyllis McMahon

Director   Kate Hewitt

Note

This should probably be a text for two voices.

The strands should begin at the same time and end within a moment or two of each other. Two lives of different lengths, but equal value.

Any moment that says 'X minutes and X seconds' should be replaced with the real time that the scene has taken to that point.

Okay.

Okay. Let's have a look.

Here we are.

she's warm
warm
warm

This is a picture of me in the womb. Isn't that incredible?

Here I am now and that's me in the womb.

warm
and then
her hair
her ears
noise
her eyes
the light
her mouth

her chin
neck
shoulders

I was born

I was born at five minutes past one in the morning.

You see that next to me in the scan?

That's my sister. My mother had been carrying twins so I actually had a sister who was born first.

arms
cold

My twin sister was born twenty minutes before I was.

torso
cold
her bottom
thighs
knees
shins
feet
her toes are out
all of her is out

She didn't survive very long sadly. She had trouble breathing. She only lived for twenty minutes.

She died almost precisely on the moment of my birth. My mum would often remind me of that.

Born at twelve forty-five a.m.

My parents never named her. I once asked why but I can't remember what the answer was.

pump
pump
pump
one hundred beats per
minute

contract
expand
contract
expand
fifty-eight breaths per
minute

pump
one hundred and four beats
per minute

contract
fifty-seven breaths per
minute

blood pumps
motion
stomach lurches
contract
expand
motion
go stomach
go throat
go arms
go legs

one minute and two
seconds
three
four
five
six hundred million bits of
information processed.

My mum would talk about my
twin sister from time to time. She
told me once about the feeling of
holding me after I was born and
then having to hold her after
she'd died. I've always
remembered that.

The same thing happened to
Elvis you know. Except his was a
twin brother.

I didn't sleep well as a baby
apparently. I cried a lot. There
I am crying.

That's my first birthday. I was a
very flatulent child. My father
always loved to bring that up.

My earliest memory is being
woken up by my father on the
sofa. I was two and a half and it
was a foggy evening and I can
still picture my pyjamas.

Oh god. That was taken when
I was three years old and my
mum caught me eating all of the
chocolates from the Christmas
tree.

My hair was very dark until the
age of four. Then it went very

one hundred and twenty
million blood cells created.
thirty thousand skin cells
shed
eighty-six billion electrical
signals sent.

contract
expand
snip
contract
hard
go mouth
blink

go arms
go legs
go vocal cords

go vocal cords

one hundred and twenty
beats per minute
fifty-seven breaths per
minute

pump
pump
pump

one hundred and twenty
beats per minute
fifty-eight breaths per
minute

one hundred and ten beats
per minute
fifty-six breaths per minute

light. Obviously you can't tell
that now.

I remember my mother taking me
to the park when I first got that
bike. Autumn. I think.

What's that one then? No idea
what's going on there.

My first day of school! I cried so
much my mother was afraid to
leave me until a teacher told her
off for mollycoddling. Look at
my mum's face. Bless her.

Now, I'm a little older there
because that's after I'd gone to
St Mary's. Look at those awful
skirts.

I wasn't badly behaved at school
but I wasn't a model student
either. I just never found it that
interesting and in those days the
teachers were, well.

I enjoyed Art but I hated French.
I enjoyed History but wasn't very
good at it.

Maths was my thing. I loved it.
Still do. I do puzzles, solve
equations, things like that. It

one hundred beats per
minute

cold
light
cold
light
noise
light
noise
noise
noise

contract
expand
pump

contract
expand
pump

ninety beats per minute
fifty-six breaths per minute

light
noise
blink
light
mouth opens
light
cold
contract
expand
contract
contract
contract

thirty breaths per minute
twenty-nine breaths per
minute
twenty-nine breaths per
minute

keeps the brain agile which is
important at my age.

My best friends at school were
called Elizabeth and Mary. There
they are. God. What was her
name? She was a part of our
gang but I can't for the life of me

Mary became a weather girl. Can
you believe that? Weather
woman, I should say. I think
Elizabeth became a nun.

After school sometimes we
would walk down to the chip
shop and each get a bag of chips.
My mum would not be
impressed.

One of the worst things I ever did
was push Mary into a bush. We
were fighting about something
and everyone laughed at her.
I felt guilty for weeks.

My first job was in the silver
service. I polished a lot of
spoons. I never liked it because
all the people there were a bit
you know. While I was working
there a man once offered a
hundred pounds if I would go
home with him. Can you believe
that!

I did my exams, of course. Maths
and Sciences.

My first proper job was working
in a shop. I did that for a year
after school. I can't think of a
single interesting story. But I did
meet my first boyfriend.

one-point-two billion bits
of information processed.
two hundred and forty
million blood cells created.
sixty thousands skin cells
shed
two hundred and two
billion electrical signals
sent.

Not long after I took up a college
course. I was the only girl on my
course. Can you believe that?

twenty-nine breaths per
minute
one hundred beats per
minute
ninety-eight beats per
minute
ninety-seven beats per
minute

When I was twenty-two I was hit
by a van going at full pelt. What
I remember most clearly was the
feeling of not being able to
breathe.

'is she okay?'

her
contract

'oh my god is she okay?'

I'd broken three ribs, fractured
my spine and my right leg was
shattered. I'd also broken my nose
as I fell and taken half the skin off
my back. I was hospitalised for
two weeks and then spent six
months in physiotherapy. I think it
was six months.

My boyfriend broke up with me
not long after I left hospital. That
hurt almost as much as the
accident. I've no idea what
happened to him.

pump

feels
feels
fire
electricity
light
noisy
pump
contract
expand
pump
noisy

It took me a long time to walk
properly again. I had to stop doing
exercise and I put weight on.

After I finished my computer
course a friend recommended me
for a job at a company called

up
motion
go stomach

Fishers. Oh I hated it there. A lot
of men talking a lot of shit.
That's us on an away day. No
idea where we are.

'Where are you taking her?'

contract
expand
pump
motion
go stomach

I met my first husband not long
after I took that job. There he is.
We were friends for a year or two
before that. I knew he liked me
but I wasn't sure if I liked him.

X minutes and X seconds
one-point-eight billion bits
of information processed.
three hundred and sixty
million blood cells created.
ninety thousand skin cells
shed
two hundred and eighty-
eight billion electrical
signals sent.

The first time we kissed? God.
I'm not sure I can remember the
very first time. I remember early
on we went on a weekend to the
country.

We went to Greece. When we
were young. Look how tired we
look.

twenty-nine breaths a
minute
thirty breaths a minute

We were together for I don't
know actually a year or so before
we found a place together. My
dad helped us with the deposit
even though he didn't really have
any money.

contract
expand
pump
contract
expand
pump
contract
expand
pump
contract
expand
pump
contract

I was the one to propose. I know!
Well I knew he'd never get round
to it. When I proposed I couldn't
get down on one knee because of
my car accident so I told him to
close his eyes and imagine that
I had.

expand
pump

ninety-six beats per minute
ninety-six beats per minute
ninety-six beats per minute

the noise
go arms
go legs
go arms and legs
go mouth
go eyelids

go lung
expands
contracts
expands
contracts

go nervous system
electric

eighty-seven beats per
minute
eighty-seven beats per
minute
eighty-eight beats per
minute
twenty-nine breaths per
minute
twenty-eight breaths per
minute

God look it that. Yes, it was a
nice wedding. I got terribly
drunk. Isn't that an awful suit?
And my hair.

Our first house. There was the
best little restaurant on our street.
I often wonder if it's still there.

My son was born in that house.
He weighed seven pounds and
eight ounces.

The birth was a nightmare. It
went on for hours and for a
period he had the umbilical chord
wrapped around his neck. He
was fine in the end but he hurt
like hell. There he is being held
by his dad.

When he was six years old my
son he was on a climbing frame
and he fell off, landing on his
head. I can still remember the
sound. I thought he was dead. He
escaped with only a few bruises
thank god.

Oh yes. For my fortieth birthday
(I think?) we went and had
dinner at one of the big hotels on
The Strand. I didn't like the food
very much but I didn't tell my
husband because it had been his
idea and we really couldn't
afford it.

It was not long after when I quit
my job and started a business
with my husband.

xxx minutes and xxx
one hundred and twenty
thousand skin cells shed.
two-point-seven billion bits
of information processed.
four hundred and eighty
million blood cells created.
one hundred and fifty
thousand skin cells shed
three hundred and fifty
billion electrical signals
sent.

motion
go stomach
air
close eyes
open eyes
go arms
go legs
go arms and legs
go mouth
go eyelids
close eyes

twenty-seven breaths per
minute
contract
expand
pump

expand
contract
expand
contract

motion
go stomach

My mother was ill for almost two
years before she died. That was
hard. This is her not long before
the end. A lot of time in hospitals
and my dad didn't cope very
well.

My dad lived for another five
years or so. He took up fishing.
He had a stroke while watching
television and was found by the
woman next door who would
water his plants. They said it
would've been very quick.

My son spoke at the funeral. He
did very well because he could
only have been about eleven or
twelve.

The business grew faster than
I could ever have hoped. It was
very exciting.

The Taj Mahal. That's for my
fiftieth! All three of us went. It's
just as beautiful up close.

This is a few years later.
I remember dropping him off at
university and looking at the
other people in his hall and
thinking god I hope they talk to
him. One of them ended up being
his best man I think.

contract
go arms
go legs
cold
noise
go vocal cords
ayhayhayh

We sold up the business. By this
point it was worth quite a lot you
know.

With our son out of the house it
was just the two of us again. We
tried, we really did. Here we are
in Greece again. It was nice but it
just wasn't the same. The only
thing we'd had in common was
go legs wave
go tongue
go vocal cords

the business and that had gone.
So.

expand
contract
pump

We stayed friends after the
divorce. Friendly anyway. He
died only about three years ago
I think and of course I went to
the funeral. His second wife gave

X minutes and X seconds

me a hug.

three billion bits of
information processed.
six hundred million blood
cells created.
one hundred and eighty
thousand skin cells shed
four hundred and thirty
billion electrical signals
sent.

I loved being single again in my
sixties. Loved it. I had
relationships with a lot of very
handsome men.

light
noise
go eyes blink
light
go mouth
go vocal cords
ayhayhayh

I had enough money never to
work again but I missed it, so
I set up a consultancy. I could
work whatever hours I wanted.
I loved it.

And then I settled down again.
This is my partner. I met him on
holiday. My son loved him. He

light
noise

go close eyes

twenty-four breaths per
minute
twenty-three breaths per
minute
twenty-four breaths per
minute

forty-two beats per minute
forty-two
forty-two
forty-one
forty-three

light
cold

contract
expand
pump
contract
expand
pump

forty-two
forty-one
forty
forty-one

three-point-eight billion
bits of information
processed.
seven hundred and twenty
million blood cells created.
two hundred and ten
thousand skin cells shed
five hundred billion
electrical signals sent.

moved into my house. This is on
his birthday.

This is our cat Steven.

We were together twelve years.
For the most part, they were
wonderful. Yes. Yes.

After he died last year I couldn't
stay in that house so I moved into
my little flat. It wasn't on the
ground floor so Steven went to
live with a friend of mine. That's
the old house just before we left
it. Doesn't it look strange without
furniture?

That's my son's wife. When he
brought her home for the first
time I wasn't very keen on her but
she's since grown on me. A bit.

They lived in Australia for a few
years. Here they are, you see.
That's where my granddaughter
was born.

I visited them twice. One time
we went camping in the outback
and I went looking for firewood.
I was lost for nearly five hours in
the dark until my son and his
friend found me.

ah
heeh
ah
yahyahyahyahyahyah

thirty-nine beats per
minute

light
light
noise
light
dark

contract
expand

twenty-four breaths per
minute.

noise
dark
lungs contract
lungs expand
noise
noise
dark

X minutes and X seconds

four-point-five billion bits
of information processed.
eight hundred and forty
million blood cells created.
two hundred and forty
thousand skin cells shed
five hundred and eighty
billion electrical signals
sent.

seventeen beats per minute

I cried like a baby. I often think
about what would have happened
if they hadn't. It was the most
frightened I've ever been in my
life.

That's what do you call it? The
Sydney Opera House.

This was the rudest waiter I've
ever met.

They're back in the UK now.
Thank god. Australia is very
beautiful but I couldn't get over
my fear of toilet spiders.

Now what's that one about?
I have no idea who that is, sorry.
I wonder why I've kept that.

I was in a book group for the
over-seventies. That's where
I met Jessica. She's the one in the
hat. She still visits me, even in
here. Although I think her
daughter has to drive her now.

Every day I would get up and
take fifteen minutes to walk to the
bus stop. I would wait for the bus,
ride it into town do my shopping
in an hour and ride the bus home.
One day when I was stepping off
the bus I misjudged the step and
fell, fracturing my forearm.

contract
noise
dark

> I had a woman come in to help me. She was very nice but we didn't have much in common. She spoke to me like I was a child, you know. She didn't know any better but it was very annoying.

expand
noise
dark

X minutes and X seconds
six hundred and thirty
billion electrical signals
sent.

> I moved in here about six months ago. The staff are very nice but I can't remember any of their names. The food is horrible but that's to be expected I suppose. I don't mind it all that much.

expand

contract

> I read a lot. My eyes are still good you know. I have the eyes of a woman ten years younger.

pump

noise
dark
noise
dark

> My son visits me once a month or so. Sometimes he brings his wife.

pump

expand

> I'm sorry I can't hear very well so you'll have to

eight beats per minute

> My arm hurts when it gets cold.

contract

noise
dark
silent
dark

> Can you plump my pillows up a bit. Thank you. No no I'm fine. There we are.

Is that it? Have we got to the end?

four beats per minute

Quite a lot, isn't it? That's quite a lot of things.

silent
dark

I'll be eighty-four next week. If I last till then.

two beats per minute

That's good enough for me.

dark

To have been through all that.

blank
blank

I feel very.

Very.

died at one-oh-four a.m.

Lucky.

PARLIAMENT SQUARE

For T.M.
The world got better.

'Courage calls to courage everywhere,
and its voice cannot be denied.'

Millicent Fawcett

Acknowledgements

Leo Butler, Mel Hillyard, Vinay Patel, Thomas Martin and Emily Wraith, all of whom encouraged me to keep going with this play when it was called something different.

The organisers, readers and judges of the Bruntwood Prize. Brian Quirt, Jenna Rodgers and everyone at the the the Banff Playwrights Colony 2016. Madani Younis, Stewart Pringle and everyone at the Bush.

Sarah Frankcom, Matthew Xia and everyone at the Royal Exchange for making me feel so at home in Manchester.

The staff at Whitechapel Ideas Store and John Harvard Library, Borough – the only two places I ever get anything done. Political, public spaces worth fighting for.

And Suzanne Bell and Jude Christian, who made this with me. The two most inspiring, patient dramaturgs a confused writer could ask for. Sorry it took me so long.

J.F.

Parliament Square was first performed at the Royal Exchange Theatre, Manchester, on 18 October 2017, before transferring to the Bush Theatre, London, on 30 November 2017. The cast was as follows:

VOICE / JO	Lois Chimimba
KAT	Esther Smith
TOMMY	Damola Adelaja
DOCTOR / ANNOUNCER / FRIEND / TAXI DRIVER	Jamie Zubairi
PHYSIO / COLLEAGUE / TICKET WOMAN / FRIEND	Kelly Hotten
MUM	Joanne Howarth
CATHERINE	Seraphina Beh

Director	Jude Christian
Designer	Fly Davis
Lighting Designer	Jack Knowles
Sound Designers	Ben & Max Ringham
Movement Director	Jennifer Jackson
Assistant Director	Amy Hailwood
Casting Directors	Jerry Knight-Smith CDG and Vicky Richardson
Stage Manager	Sophie Tetlow
Deputy Stage Manager	Hannah Phillips

118

Characters

KAT
TOMMY
TAXI DRIVER
TICKET WOMAN
COLLEAGUE
MUM
DOCTOR
CATHERINE
PHYSIO
FRIEND
FRIEND 2
JO

Note

The two columns of text in Fifteen Seconds are both part of Kat.
How you interpret and stage that is totally up to you.

A line with no full stop at the end indicates an unfinished
thought.

A dash at the end of a line indicates an interruption. A dash at the
beginning indicates someone halfway through a sentence.

ONE

FIFTEEN SECONDS

                                                          Kat.

…

                                                    Get up.

                                                          Kat.

…

                                                GET UP.

What?

                                              The alarm.

What time?

                                    Turn off the alarm.

Dreaming.

                                        Before he wakes.

Why – ?

Oh.

                                                  Today.

Today is –

                                    Today is THE day.

                                    You slept so well.

Didn't think I

                                Didn't think you would but

Need to get up.

                                      Don't wake him.

Nothing wakes him.

                                        He's a log.

A lump.

                                    Fifteen seconds.

Fifteen seconds.

That's all I have to get through and then –

                                    Get out of bed.

This is the –

                        Don't think like that get out of bed.

Love these pillows.

                            They're very soft get out of bed.

This bed.

                            It's very nice get out of bed.

One more minute.

                                            Now.

Just one more.

                            I am not fucking about.

One –

            Get up! Get up! Get up! Get up! Get up! Get up!
                        GEEEEEET UUUUUUP!

I'm up. I'm up.

                                        Great job.

God.

                                We're on the way.

On the way.

                                    Can you feel it?

I can feel it. My stomach.

                            You can feel it and it feels

He's fast asleep.

Good.

Look at him.

That face.

Want to wake him.

Come on.

Say hello.

Don't be thick.

I'm not thick.

The drawer.

You're thick.

Softly.

Top. Jeans.

Those ones.

They'll do.

They're fine.

Except. Maybe?

No.

I mean they're not very –

No.

I know what you're doing.

What?

Delaying.

I'm not.

Delaying the moment you have to –

I just think this top isn't very –

Just take the fucking clothes.

Okay.

Well done.

Now. Out the room.

Okay.

But.

Maybe I should just wake him.

No.

Say something.

Can't just leave him without –

You have to.

He looks so lovely.

Tommy.

My lovely husband.

He's drooling.

He is! He's drooling in his sleep!

On his chin.

Done that since he was a teenager oh bless him.

Look at him.

He's so

disgusting.

Beautiful.

Such a beautifully disgusting man.

I love him so much.

Do you?

Yeah I do yeah I really do.

Okay.

God. I'm gonna miss him. I'm gonna
miss you Tommy.

Oh.

You won't.

I will.

You won't.

Our own little world.

That's what we're like. That's what
Mum always says.

She says a lot of things.

She does yeah.

Come on.

**You think hanging around is gonna
make it easier to go through with this?**

Should say goodbye.

Don't be thick.

Stop saying that.

He'll know something's wrong.

How will he –

He can sense these things on you.

I'm a good liar.

You're a shit liar.

I'm a shit liar.

Stick to the plan.

I want to speak to him.

**Stick to the fucking
plan you idiot.**

**If he gets even a sniff of what
you're planning he'll lock you up
before he lets you leave the house.**

Maybe I need that.

No.

You got that will-I-won't-I shit out your system weeks ago and now you're ready aren't you?

Wait. He's moving.

Oh shit.

Oh my god he's waking up.

What do I –

TOMMY. *Kat? What time is it?*

I got to go in early today.

Hold it together.

TOMMY. *Why?*

Hold it together.

Team meeting.

He believes you.

TOMMY. *That's shit innit?*

Didn't mean to wake you. Go back to sleep.

Well done.

Can I give him a

Yeah. Okay.

Kiss him.

TOMMY. *Have a nice day.*

  I'll see you later.

Say it back.

See you later.

Good.

TOMMY. *Love you.*

Say it.

Love you too.

He's closed his eyes.

Take a moment.

**You're okay. You're strong enough.
You can take this.**

Am I?

You're doing so well.

Oh. Oh.

Fifteen seconds.

That's all you have to get through.

I can do that.

**Course you can because you're
a fucking amazing woman.**

Am I?

You are.

Am I yeah I am.

Thank you.

You're fucking welcome.

Downstairs.

Downstairs. I'm doing this.

You're doing this.

Although –

Wait.

No.

Wait I can't just.

No no.

Jo.

Don't do this to me.

Jo Jo. I can't just go without
saying goodbye to her.

You decided against this.

I know.

Decided it was too hard.

I know I did but

It's torture.

I'll be alright. I promise.

Oh you promise?

I won't wake her up.

So long as you promise.

I'll just. Look at her.

It's a bad idea.

I'm doing it.

It's an awful idea.

I'll be fine. Bedroom. I'll be fine.

Careful.

There she is.

Don't wake her up.

Jo. Hiya Jo.

Quietly.

Ohhh I love her.

She's dreaming.

I'm leaving her.

She'll understand.

She's gonna hate me.

When she's old enough.
She'll get it.

I can't.

Be proud of who her mum is.

I'm a terrible person.

You are the best person.

Look at her.

I can't.

This is the best thing for her.

Hold on to that.

Let's go, eh?

What if I take her with me?

Say goodbye.

I could though couldn't I?
I could take her with me.

Say goodbye.

I could take her with me or
maybe I could I could I could

Say goodbye.

Oh   god.

Please.

  Goodbye.

Well done.

Oww.

Owwwwwww.

That was hard.

Oh shut up.

I know that was hard.

Just shut the fuck up please.

But time is ticking.

I need a minute.

You haven't got a minute.

IF I SAY I WANT A MINUTE
I CAN TAKE A MINUTE.

Alright.

…

That's probably enough now.

Time to get going.

I'm gonna be sick.

No you're not.

Okay. Okay.

You're ready.

Out the front door.

I can't.

It's not gonna get any easier.

This house all that time the
things that have happened
the day we moved in the parties
the evenings on the sofa the sex
on the stairs my birthday in the
kitchen pizza and telly in bed

Stop.

The day we came home with her from the hospital.

Leave.

Bye.

Well done.

Forward. That's it.

Garden path. Front gate.

Down the street.

What will the neighbours say
tomorrow? Imagine.

Jesus. I'm doing this

Yeah you are!

I'm doing this.

You're doing this.

I'M DOING THIS!

YOU'RE A SUPERSTAR!

I'M A SUPERSTAR!

Taxi.

There!

Hiya. Station please.

Relax.

My stomach.

TAXI DRIVER. *Want the radio on?*

Answer him.

Okay.

He knows something.

Ridiculous.

He can tell something's wrong
the way he's looking at me.

Calm down.

He knows he knows what
I've got in my bag.

How could he?

TAXI DRIVER. *What time's your train?*

I. I don't know.

Keep calm keep quiet.

I should've walked.

You're fine. Look out the window.

Should've got the bus he knows
he knows I can tell he's gonna stop
me gonna tell someone this is taking
too long I don't know this route it's
too hot in here I need to get out get him
to pull over –

TAXI DRIVER. *Here we are.*

That's eight pound forty.

Keep the change.

Deep breath.

The station.

The last time we were here.
Holiday. All these people.

Nobody's looking.

Police.

What if they ask to look in my bag?

Why would they?

Don't worry.

I'm not worried.

Alright.

I'm not worried.

Ticket office.

Hi. Could I get a ticket to

TICKET WOMAN. *One way or return?*

One way please.

TICKET WOMAN. *One hundred and
    thirty-five pounds please.*

Is she fucking joking?

That sounds like a lot.

Have a heart attack. Have a stroke.

TICKET WOMAN. *It's the price of a peak ticket.
    If you want to wait until 9 a.m. ...*

So smug I hate her.

**Stand your ground! Tell her there's no
way you're paying that!**

Should I?!

No we've got somewhere to be.

TICKET WOMAN. *Do you want the ticket or not?*

Just pay it.

It's not just my money it's Tommy's money it's –

Grit your teeth.

Yes please.

**That's right. You give her an angry stare.
That'll show her.**

Think about tomorrow.

**When she sees the news in a few hours
she's gonna feel so guilty. She'll be eating
her lunch and she'll recognise
you the girl who came to her counter
and she'll realise what you were on your way**

> **to do and she'll feel guilty she didn't give**
> **you the off-peak fare.**
>
> **She'll spend the rest of her life telling**
> **people that she served you on the day**
> **that it happened and she'll be grateful she'll be**
> **so grateful that she served you.**
>
> **She served you on the day that you –**

TICKET WOMAN. *Excuse me.*
  There's a queue behind you.

> **Take your ticket.**

Thank you.

> **Fuck you.**

TICKET WOMAN. *Platform number eight.*

Here we go.

> **Take a breath. That's it.**
> **Take your time.**

Just a normal woman. A normal
woman walking through the
station normally.

Seat to myself.

> **Relax.**

We're moving.

> **You're hungry.**

No.

> **Eat something.**

I wonder if they're awake yet.

> **Probably not.**

Wonder how long it will take him
to realise I'm not at work?

> **Might be a while.**
> **He can be a bit slow.**

COLLEAGUE. *Kat?*

Shit.

COLLEAGUE. *Kat!*

Ignore her. Look the other way.

COLLEAGUE. *Thought that was you.*
What you doing on here?

Oh hiya. Didn't see you.

COLLEAGUE. *I was waving right at you,*
you were in your own little world.
Not working today then? Me neither
I'm not in all week now, lucky for us eh,
that place'll fall apart without us there you
watch, although can't get much worse can it?

Brian never said you were having time off,
where d'you say you were off to?

I didn't. Visiting family.

COLLEAGUE. *That's nice.*

Be specific.

My aunt's sixty-seventh birthday.

The fuck did that come from?

COLLEAGUE. *Ohhh how nice.*

You don't even have an aunt.

COLLEAGUE. *Tommy not coming?*

No. No he's staying behind.
Looking after Jo. I should –

COLLEAGUE. *Aww. How's she doing little angel?*

She's.

Fine. Yeah.

COLLEAGUE. *Bet you're gonna miss her.*
Always hard leaving them behind at that age.

I. Yeah.

It's alright.

COLLEAGUE. *Remember it well. Didn't*
want to be away from my Peter for
a second when he was two. You feel it
don't you? Instinct kicks in. Course now
he's fifteen I can't wait to get away from him.

Hey. Look at you. You're shaking.

I'm sorry.

COLLEAGUE. *She'll be fine.*
You're not away long are you?

No. Sorry. Not feeling well.

COLLEAGUE. *Here this'll cheer you up.*

Oh no.

COLLEAGUE. *I've told you that*
we're getting a conservatory put in.

Only every bloody day.

COLLEAGUE. *They finished work*
this week that's what it looks like.

Very nice.

COLLEAGUE. *Well it's not much*
but we love it. Somewhere to sit
and read the paper.

What's in the bag?

Sorry?

COLLEAGUE. *In the bag? A present*
for your auntie?

Tell her.

That's right.

Tell her what it is.

See what she says.

It's a. A.

**Well if you're not gonna tell the
truth at least say something.**

A.

Been a very long silence now.

A toolbox.

**Toolbox? For your
auntie's birthday?**

COLLEAGUE. *Oh. Right. Bit of a DIY
nut is she?*

Yes. She is.

COLLEAGUE. *Toolbox wouldn't
be much use to my Bill. He wouldn't
know one end of a hammer from the other.*

I can't do this.

Breathe.

She's so

I know.

Never shuts up. At work.
Always poking her nose in to
everyone's business always blathering
away about nothing in particular
did you see have you heard so-and-so
said my son Peter

And her conservatory.

And her conservatory you'd think
it was the Sistine fucking Chapel the
way she goes on about it on and on she
goes just blathering chattering away
'*Oooh I know isn't it awful.*' As if that's enough.
Every day every fucking day. We go in and we
work and we talk shit and we all go home and
sit on our sofas and watch it all happen
because it's nothing to do with

It's nothing to do with us.

Maybe I should tell her what I'm gonna do.

You could.

I could, couldn't I?

Imagine her face.

She wouldn't believe you.

She might.

She'd have a heart attack.

Might be impressed.

Might want to do it too.

COLLEAGUE. *Want a biscuit Kat?*

Ooh a biscuit.

COLLEAGUE. *They're a bit melted but
    they taste alright.*

No thanks.

I want a biscuit!

COLLEAGUE. *I'm going to go to
    the coffee man. Would you like anything?*

You're thirsty.

No thank you.

Ask for some water.

I'm fine.

COLLEAGUE. *Okay, if you're sure.*

Thank you.

You know what?
She's actually pretty nice.

Yeah.

She is.

I feel a bit bad now.

                                    You should feel bad.

                                         What's that?

It's Tommy.

                                           Oh shit.

What do I do?

                           You knew he was going to call.

What do I do?

                                    Turn the phone off.

Decline.

                                      He'll keep trying.

A voicemail.

                                         Don't listen.

TOMMY. *Kat? It's me.*

                                      Or just ignore me.

TOMMY. *Work rang and they said
    you've not come in. So. Just
    wondering where you've got to.
    Give me a call back when you get this.
    Love you bye.*

That's it. That's all he said.

                                       Fifteen seconds.

She's coming back.

                                      Close your eyes.

                                 Pretend to be asleep.

                                           That's –

COLLEAGUE. *Kat?*

    Kat we're here.

                                            What?

COLLEAGUE. *Didn't want to wake you*
  you looked so peaceful.

Oh you actually fell asleep.

COLLEAGUE. *You slept the whole way!*

Sorry.

COLLEAGUE. *Don't you apologise.*
  I know what it's like when they're young.
  I'll see you back at work next week I spose?

Yeah. Next week.

Careful.

COLLEAGUE. *Enjoy your family do.*

I'm not

What you doing?

I'm not going to a family do.

Oh my –

COLLEAGUE. *I don't understand.*

I lied before.

COLLEAGUE. *Oh. Right.*

She looks so sad.

I'm going to Parliament Square.

Come on.

COLLEAGUE. *Okay.*

I'm gonna stand in the square,
stand in front of that building and

Don't do this.

and take a photo.

COLLEAGUE. *Right.*

Well.

Have a nice time.

What was that about?

Sorry.

Get off the train.

Not been here for years.

I don't remember any of this.

Underground.

So many people.

**You're gonna make things
better for all of them.**

So many.

**So many people and they're all gonna
know your name tomorrow that's –**

*I'm sorry ladies and gentlemen
we're going to be held here due
to a passenger incident on the
tracks up ahead.*

Passenger incident?

Look at their faces.

Person under a train he means.

Late for their meetings.

All those people on that platform
and no one could stop them doing it.
It's so hot in here.

A body under a train. Imagine that.
Imagine seeing that.

Don't think about it.

Imagine being that person.
Would it hurt? Would you feel
it happening?

I said don't think about it.

Or would it just go black would
everything just go black oh god
I'm hot I'm so hot –

Calm down.

I can't breathe.

I'm gonna be sick I've got
to get off.

This isn't our stop?

I've got to get off I've got to
get off now.

Alright go.

Oh god I'm gonna be

Quickly find a

Hooooaah

Lovely.

Oh.

Right on the platform.

You alright mate?

I'm okay. I need air.

Get above ground.

Don't forget your bag!

Fresh air. Breathe. What's that?

Mum.

Don't answer it.

Don't answer it I'm warning you.

Hi Mum.

Dunno why I bother.

MUM. *Hi love. Won't keep you,*
  I've just got a quick question
  about the weekend.

The weekend.

She doesn't know you're gone.

MUM. *Wondered if you lot*
    wouldn't mind coming a bit early,

Hasn't spoken to him.

MUM. *at about two-ish so that*
    Tommy can help me get the barbecue going.

The barbecue.

MUM. *Yes love you know I hate doing it*
    and he did such a good job last time
    and I want it nice and hot by the time
    everyone arrives. I know we said later
    but two would really help me out.

    So two then, on Saturday? I've bought
    far too much food.

Two. That's fine.

MUM. *Lovely. Everything else okay*
    with you?

Yes. Mum, it's –

MUM. *Okay love got to go.*
    See you Saturday. Bye.

Careful.

Bye. Mum.

Sit down.

I –

You should sit down.

Breathe.

She –

She'll know soon enough.

We should keep going.

I'm tired.

I know.

I'm really tired now.

**One foot in front of the other
that's all you need to do now
one foot in front of the –**

No. No. No.

TOMMY. *Kat. Did you get my last message?*
You're still not at work. Getting a bit worried
now. Give me a ring back.

Kat what the hell do you think you're doing?
You can't just get up and go and not say anything.

Stop.

TOMMY. *Please Kat, call back.*
I'll keep trying.

Stop listening to them.

TOMMY. *Jesus Kat where… where are you.*
I'm starting to really worry now.

Kat, I love you. Please just call me.
I don't care where you are or what
you're doing I just want you to call me.
Please. Jo and me, we're worried about you.

Jo. My little Jo. I wonder if she knows?

How could she?

When she grows up

**Don't think about it
what are you doing?**

When she grows up I wonder
who'll she'll be?

You fucking idiot.

I wonder who her new mum will be?

> **Shut up shut up I won't
> let you do this.**

What am I doing?

Oh god what am I doing?

Things are good for me. Got a job.
Got a husband who loves me.
A beautiful little girl. Got enough
money to eat, to heat my home.

Got a barbecue at my mum's on Saturday.

> **So what?**

Why me? Why do I have to do it?

> **Why not? There's a reason why
> you haven't been able to stop –**

There are other people.

Other ways.

> **They tried with their anger
> their marches their speeches you saw
> them thousands on the streets and
> then what happened? What?**

I could do something else.

> **There's nothing else.**

I could say something give a speech.

> **A speech? From you?**

Yes.

> **Okay.**

I could write a good speech.

> **Sure thing. I'm sure everybody
> would be queueing up to hear that one.**

> **Who's gonna listen to what you've
> got to say? You're no one.**

I'm not no one.

I'm a a woman.

> **A woman? What kind of answer is that?**

A mum.

> **Everyone's a fucking mum.**
> **What else you got?**

Fuck you.

> **Fuck you.**
> **You might as well have not been born.**

No.

That's not true.

> **You're absolutely right.**
> **And you know why?**
> **Because you're gonna do this.**
> **Do something that lasts.**

Yes. Okay.

> **You want to change things.**

I do I really do.

> **Then come on!**

Come on!

> **Come on!**

COME ON!

> **Feel that?**

I feel it!

> **Feel that inside?**

Yeah I do I fucking do.

> **Focus on that focus on that anger**
> **with what's happening that's what**

                                   **will drive you that's what's gonna
                                            get you over the line.**

Yes!

                              **Do this and the whole world will listen
                              they will realise that they can't just stand
                                          by any more. Your face is
                                       gonna go around the world.**

                              **It'll be a beacon of hope on every screen
                              and everyone will be talking about it.**

                                       Your name will ring out.

                                          IT WILL RING OUT.

                                       It will mean something.

                                                 Because.

Because.

I'm going through with it.

                                                      Yes.

                                                    Again.

I'm going through with it.

                                                  Louder.

I'M GOING THROUGH WITH IT
I'M GOING THROUGH WITH IT
I'M GOING THROUGH WITH IT!

                                              It's nice right?

                                     How calm you feel now?

I do. I do feel calm.

                                         Look at the map.

I can walk from here.

                              One foot in front of the other.

                                                    Look.

There.

A post box.

Oh. I almost forgot.

Take out the letter.

Maybe I should check it over?

Make sure it's okay.

You've read it a hundred times.
It's perfect. Post it.

It will work. Won't it?

Of course it will.

It explains everything.

Yes. It does.

Post it. Quick. Before –

It's gone.

Well done.

That's the last thing.

Almost.

It's starting to rain.

Oh my god it's really coming down.

Keep going.

Didn't bring a jacket why didn't I bring
a jacket I'm drenched I'm –

It doesn't matter.

Ugh!

Almost there.

MUM. *Kat, love, it's your mum.*
I just spoke to Tommy. Just give us
a call back to let us know where you are.
We're all a bit worried.

Up ahead.

I can barely see it through the rain.

**Keep going. Here.
You're here.**

I don't remember it looking like this.
Did it always look like this?

Cross the road.

There's not many people. So many cars.

Oh. Where do I do it?

By the statues?

In the middle of the square?

I don't know.

I don't know.

**You really should've thought
about this before.**

It's Tommy again.

Don't answer.

**Don't do it I'm warning you
don't you dare don't you
dare answer that fucking phone.**

Hi Tommy.

TOMMY. *Jesus Christ, Kat. Thank god
you're alright. Where are you? I've
been so worried.*

Parliament Square.

TOMMY. *What? What the hell are you doing there?
What's that noise?*

It's raining.

TOMMY. *Listen. It doesn't matter.
Just get back on a train and come
home, eh?*

I'm. I'm sorry but. I can't.

TOMMY. *Okay just find somewhere safe
    and I'll come and get you.*

No.

TOMMY. *Kat please. I'm coming to get you.*

No don't. I'm not coming home so

TOMMY. *What's going on Kat? You're
    really scaring me now.*

I'm sorry.

TOMMY. *We love you. I love you.*

I love you too.

TOMMY. *Then come home eh? Get on
    a train and come back here where it's
    warm and dry and we can talk about it,
    talk through whatever's bothering you.*

I'm so sorry. I have to.

TOMMY. *Kat –*

    Come back home to me and Jo.

                        That's enough now.

I'm. Bye Tommy.

                        Throw the phone away.

Okay.

                        Well done.

Owwww.
Owwwwwwwwwwwwwwwwwwwwwwwwwwwww.

                        I know.

                        You should get started.

                        Go into your bag.

Take it out.

The petrol.

Fifteen seconds.

**Fifteen seconds until the fire
burns through the nerve endings
and then you don't feel anything.**

You can count it in your head.

I'm scared.

I'm scared.

I'm really scared.

I'm really scared.

It's gonna hurt.

Fifteen seconds.

It's gonna hurt so much.

**Fifteen seconds and then imagine.
Don't you want to know what it feels like?
What it looks like.**

**The fire the flames.
Your last experience your most exciting.**

I don't.

I don't.

I don't want to die.

I don't want to die.

You could just not.

I could.

**You could put down the petrol can
and walk away.**

I could.

Go home. Kiss him. Watch telly.

Have a bath. Have sex. Eat a lasagne.

Go to your daughter's school.
Go to your daughter's wedding.

My daughter's –

Jo. Jo.

Yes. I could. I could couldn't I –

But you're not going to.

No. I'm not going to.

Say the words.

I'm going through with this.

The hard part's over.

I'm excited. I'm so excited!

The hard part?

Fifteen seconds.

Look around you.

Take it all in.

Road. Grass. Parliament. Cars. Rain on my face.

Oh my god.

I just. A memory. Came here as
a kid with Mum. We stood right
over there and she took a photo.

Breathe.

Got an ice cream and took the
boat down the river.

Breathe.

Take it all in.

Rain. Wind. Concrete. Suits. Cars.
Traffic lights. A fence. A Tesco.
I can see a fucking Tesco!

Of course a fucking Tesco's
one of the last things that I'll see.

What else?

Statues. Oh god. Police. Flagpoles.
Jo. Her face.

What else?

Clouds. Oh god.

What else?

People. Tommy's face. Jo's fingers.
Jo's eyes her smell. People on the street.

Looking?

They're huddled from the rain they're
looking down they're rushing by.

Okay.

Ready?
Think it's time.

One. More. Second.

One more.

Now or never.

Wind. My face.

Get it over with.

Okay. Okay.

Petrol can.

My hands.

Lid.

Smell.

Tip it.

It stinks!

All over.

Stings.

That's enough.

Deep breath.

Deep breath.

You're a hero.

The lighter.

Where is it?

Can't find my lighter –

Top pocket.

Take it out.

The last thing you'll ever touch.

How does it feel in your hand?

It –

I mean it feels like a fucking lighter.

You're alright.

I'm fine.

Doing great.

You are so brave.

Everyone –

The first fifteen seconds. That's all.

**Count to fifteen and it will
be just like**

Going to sleep.

You. Are. Everything.

Ready?

Yes.

1

2

3

go.

She's on fire.

Fifteen seconds.

My eyes!

One.

Two.

Three

Four.

Hold. On.

Jo.

Five.

Hold on.

Six.

Don't.

Seven.

Scream.

Eight.

She screams.

It is the worst scream we've ever heard.

TWO

FIFTEEN STEPS

Dark.

Silent.

Nothing.

And then.

...

Loud.

Bright.

KAT. *On a bed.*

Her breath rattles and her body shakes violently into life as the whole world shakes violently into life.

What seems like thousands of doctors, nurses, paramedics, anaesthetists buzzing round shouting.

KAT *screams.*

Black.

...

And then. Sunlight.

A hospital room. KAT *on the bed, alone. Her eyes open.*

They close.

Black.

...

Open. TOMMY *and* MUM *look on.* KAT *isolated. Silent.*

TOMMY. Did she. Did she say anything to you?

Anything that might explain –

A moment.

MUM. No.

TOMMY. What do I –

Close.

...

Eyes open. MUM, TOMMY *and a* DOCTOR.

DOCTOR. – the body shunts all the blood and fluid to the burned area. But when it gets there there's no skin to hold it in, so it leaks out, and without that fluid the kidneys and heart can be in serious danger of giving out.

MUM. Oh Jesus.

DOCTOR. Quick work on arrival meant we were able to get that fluid into her, and get those burns excised early on, which is key to stopping the body going into shock.

So far we've been able to counter any signs of infection. Her temperature's come right down. She's strong your daughter.

MUM. She is.

TOMMY. How. What's she going to look like? When the bandages come off?

DOCTOR.Well. Kat's burns are very severe. The use of the petrol on top of her clothes has resulted in some very deep burns, particularly on parts of the torso and the right arm and leg. After what her body's been through, she's lucky to even be alive. If the fire hadn't been put out so quickly –

MUM. The police said it was just a young girl with her jacket. Did you know that?

DOCTOR. I heard.

MUM. What have they got covering her?

DOCTOR. It's a temporary covering until she's strong enough for the first of the skin grafts.

MUM. It looks so. Strange.

DOCTOR. Well. It's cadaver skin.

TOMMY. A dead body. They've got her covered in a dead man's skin.

Close.

...

Open. TOMMY *alone.*

He doesn't know where to put his hands. Close.

...

Open. KAT *looks around but they don't notice.*

MUM. – on a short-term let. It's no palace, but it'll do. It'll get us out that B and B at least. If I have to talk to that woman one more time.

TOMMY. I still don't see why they can't move her closer to home.

Let me give you some money at least.

MUM. Absolutely not.

Close.

...

Open.

MUM. Oh my god.

Did you see that?

Her eyes her eyes were open.

TOMMY. I didn't see.

MUM. They were Kat love Kat it's me can you –

Close.

...

Open.

DOCTOR. Kat? Kat can you hear me?

TOMMY. Oh my god.

MUM. Oh Kat. Hiya.

TOMMY. Oh my god thank you god thank you.

MUM. I told you, didn't I?

Believe. You've got to keep believing.

...

TOMMY. So.

Jo's fine. She's at my sister's.

You've been out of it for weeks.

There was a moment where we thought –

You should see us. Me and your mum, in this funny little flat together, 'bout half-hour away. I haven't killed her yet, somehow.

Jo. She. She doesn't know what's gone on. Obviously. She knows something's up. But. I'll bring her down when you're feeling a bit better eh?

God I love you. You gave me such a fright.

...

MUM. I fucking hate hospitals.

If I have to have another sandwich from that café.

Call me old-fashioned but I don't think it counts as bacon if it's grey.

Count yourself lucky you're being fed through a drip. There's your silver lining eh?

KAT. M. Mum.

MUM. Hey. Don't worry. Doctor says you're gonna get out of here. We'll get you home.

Once you've had your skin graft and they've started physio.

You scared the shit out of me. Do you know that? Thought we'd lost you. You silly girl.

You were so lucky. If that girl hadn't been there.

KAT. Mum. Did it.

Did it. Work?

MUM. No. No Kat you're still here. Don't worry. You're still alive.

KAT. No.

My letter.

I. I sent you. A letter.

MUM. Get some rest eh?

I'm gonna ask them about getting you a plant or something. Brighten the place up.

...

MUM. You should be very proud you know, Catherine.

CATHERINE. Yeah?

MUM. Young girl like you. Bet your mum's so proud of you.

CATHERINE. Dunno about that.

MUM. Even a moment longer.

CATHERINE. Just glad I was there. I was only a few feet from her I don't think she spotted me. Saw her take out the petrol.

MUM. Okay.

CATHERINE. Splash it on herself. And I was like what is she doing?

MUM. Well.

CATHERINE. You can't just let people die you know. That's what I think anyway. Life's important, innit?

Was funny. Soon as I saw her take the lighter out something in my head just went GO. Like someone else was driving me. You ever get that?

Straight over got my jacket around her didn't even think about it.

Bit of my hair burnt off. Didn't even notice. Adrenalin you know fight or flight. Like you always wonder what you'd be like in those situations don't you and I guess now I know.

MUM. Well you're certainly in our prayers. I mean we're not religious. But you would be. If we were. I don't know why I said that. I'm just gonna hug you.

CATHERINE. Alright!

MUM. I was saying to Tommy. They should give you an award.

CATHERINE. An award.

For me?

No… I mean. Maybe.

MUM. I don't see why not.

You're a hero. How many people would do what you did.

CATHERINE. I did think there was gonna be more about it you know? In the news. Girl saves burning woman or something but –

I looked and couldn't find anything. Not that that's why I did it. But. It would have been nice to have something to show people, you know?

MUM. Your jacket.

It put out the flames.

Must be ruined.

CATHERINE. Oh yeah it's fucked.

MUM. Let me give you some money for it.

CATHERINE. That's okay.

MUM. You're young you need the money. How much was it?

CATHERINE. Don't worry about it.

MUM. Seriously.

CATHERINE. It's fine.

MUM. I want to.

CATHERINE. Two hundred quid.

MUM. For a jacket?

That's. Okay of course that's fine.

CATHERINE. Oh that's so nice. Thank you.

Can I ask you something?

Hope you don't think I'm rude but

Since it happened it's been going round and round my head and I need to ask.

Why'd she do it?

MUM. What d'you mean?

CATHERINE. Like, why?

MUM. There wasn't a reason.

CATHERINE. Musta been something.

MUM. No.

CATHERINE. So she just did it?

MUM. There's no good reason when someone does something like this.
She's not well. That's all.

CATHERINE. Oh. Okay.

Why there though? That's all I was wondering. Why that spot?

MUM. Maybe you should come back when she's a bit more with it, eh?

...

DOCTOR. Hi Kat.

How are you doing today?

I must say we're all very pleased to see you up and awake.

KAT. It hurts.

DOCTOR. Now let me take a look here. And here. Very good. That's good.

This is gonna be a bit.

KAT. Ah!

DOCTOR. A bit sore. There we go. All looks okay to me. You're doing very well. You'll get out of here soon, I promise.

If it helps.

I just wanted to.

What you did.

I mean I'm not really supposed to say anything like this but.

The stuff we see. Put up with. Working here.

The country feels. Sick. And so when I heard about what happened to you.

I understand. I get why. A lot of us here do.

Just thought you should know that. Thought it might help.

Okay.

Now Kat, I'm going to continue checking your dressings, alright? You're going to have to be very brave for me.

DOCTOR *continues checking* KAT*'s dressing.* KAT *cries. It is the most painful feeling in the world.*

...

TOMMY. Jo's being as good as gold apparently.

KAT. Jo.

TOMMY. I'll bring her in soon. I promise.

We thought we'd wait until you were feeling up to it before we brought her.

They said I should take some pictures of you. To show her. To help her adjust so it's not so much of a shock when she –

Maybe later eh?

KAT. Tommy –

TOMMY. So you know. I've told people back home you had an accident. Cooking.

KAT. What. Why?

TOMMY. I've been thinking and.

I don't want you to tell me why you did this.

I don't want us to talk about that.

Ever. Okay?

I won't ask you. And I don't want you to tell me. Because I can't –

Okay.

Let's just get you better.

...

KAT. Mum. I haven't seen anything. In the news.

MUM. Well. You seem perkier.

KAT. What's going on has anything happened?

MUM. You've been in here for weeks. Lots has happened.

There's nothing to worry about if that's what you mean.

KAT. People saw me people must have seen me.

MUM. You were lucky the whole thing didn't last for very long.

KAT. No. No no.

Mum I posted you a letter explaining. Asking you to tell people. Tell Tommy. But he doesn't

MUM. There was no letter love. I'm sorry. Are you sure you aren't confused?

KAT. No!

MUM. The doctors say that you might be a bit confused about events that day.

KAT. No no no this doesn't make sense.

I need to get out of here.

MUM. Settle down.

KAT. I need to get out help me get out. I need to tell people.

I need to

I need to

KAT *breaks.*

MUM *holds her daughter.*

...

PHYSIO. Hiya Kat.

How you feeling today?

Nothing? That's okay I get that a lot.

So I thought I'd come say hi as I'm going to be doing physio with you twice a day over the next few weeks. I know right. Lucky you.

See this face? Nice innit. Get a good look because in a few days you're gonna hate it. It's alright, I won't take it personally. You're gonna hate this face because it's going to make you do a lot of things that you don't want to do. A lot of things that are going to be quite painful. But it's only through doing those things that we're gonna get you up and about alright? Get you walking.

I'm going to need you to believe in me and trust that I know what I'm doing. Can you do that Kat? Work through the pain, work together, and we'll get you to the end of this.

...

TOMMY. I'm going back home. I need to be back at work and.

My sister's had Jo too long and.

And I can't be here any more Kat. I'm sorry but I just. Can't.

I think if I stay I won't be able to stop myself asking why. And that's. That's not.

Because I've tried not to get angry.

Get upset.

But. You got up. And you left me. Without saying a word. Without even saying goodbye.

One moment I thought things were fine and the next you're on the phone and.

And that's why I'm gonna go. For a bit. So I can. Think. You know? Calm down. Because I want to help you get through this. I do.

Life is a very

I mean it's a gift isn't it? That's what they say and

This world. Well. It's not so bad is it? There's actually a lot of good in it. If you look. There's value in all of our lives. That's what I think anyway.

And I think. Hope. That we can be. That I can still make you. Happy.

And so it doesn't matter why you did this. What matters is

Anyway. I love you.

I'll be back soon.

...

PHYSIO. How are we doing today? Feeling good? Ready to get started on some physio!?

No?

Nothing? Just gonna leave me stood here talking to myself? That's fine.

I find myself pretty charming company actually.

Hello mate how are you today I'm fine thanks for asking.

I can wait all day.

Well not all day I have other appointments.

But a while. I can wait a while.

Okay. We'll try again tomorrow.

...

DOCTOR. Where's your lovely husband then? Haven't seen him in a few days.

KAT. Please. You said you understood why I did. What I did.

DOCTOR. I'm sorry?

KAT. You told me you understood.

Nobody knows that it happened. Can you help me? Maybe you can contact a journalist or –

DOCTOR. Oh. Um. I don't think that would be.

KAT. Or you could take a photo and share it maybe?

DOCTOR. That's not really allowed I'm afraid.

KAT. But you said –

DOCTOR. I think you're mixing me up with someone else.

Listen. I'm really sorry. I would if I could.

Keep up your physio. Keep working.

You'll be out of here in no time.

...

PHYSIO. Right Kat. What's say we try again eh?

KAT. I'm sleeping.

PHYSIO. You can sleep. You can stay in that bed forever if you like. Well maybe not that bed. We need that bed. But a bed. Somewhere.

Or I can get you up and you can get on with the rest of your life.

Get you walking again. It's up to you.

You want to get out of here don't you?

There must be something you want to do out there? Right?

Something you want to achieve?

There is.

KAT. Yes.

PHYSIO. What is it?

That's fine you don't have to tell me.

Just so long as you're ready to get started.

Okay.

...

KAT. I can't I can't do it I don't want to do it.

PHYSIO. I know you don't but I'm gonna make you so…

KAT. Ohhhh I fucking hate you.

PHYSIO. I hate you back. Three steps.

KAT. Fuck you.

PHYSIO. Fuck you.

>   Three steps. One. That's it. Two.

>   From there to me. Come on. Come on!

>   Three. Well done. Well done you.

...

KAT. Seven?

PHYSIO. Seven.

KAT. I thought it was three.

PHYSIO. It was three yesterday.

KAT. No.

PHYSIO. It's seven today.

KAT. No way.

PHYSIO. Seven today fifteen by the end of the week.

KAT. I'm not doing seven you can shove seven up your arse.

PHYSIO. That was the deal. Three yesterday. Seven today.

KAT. And fifteen. It'll take me months to get to fifteen.

PHYSIO. End of the week. Come on.

KAT. It's too many.

PHYSIO. One.

KAT. God.

PHYSIO. Two.
    Three. That's it.

KAT. It hurts.
    Just let me. Rest here for a second.

PHYSIO. You're doing so well.

>   Come on. Four!

KAT. Why do you do this?

PHYSIO. It's my job.

KAT. That's not an answer.
I won't keep going until you tell me.

PHYSIO. Come on.

KAT. Fine. I'm done. Four steps is enough.

PHYSIO. Alright. You really want to know?
I'm going to ask you a question.

KAT. Ask away.

PHYSIO. It's going to sound quite blunt.

KAT. Okay.

PHYSIO. And I don't expect you to say yes.

KAT. That's fine.

PHYSIO. Have you accepted the Lord Jesus Christ as your
personal saviour?

KAT. Oh my god you're one of them.

PHYSIO. It's just a question.

KAT. Nurse! Nurse!

PHYSIO. You don't have to say yes.
I'm not here to convert you.

KAT. No I haven't accepted Jesus as my personal saviour.

PHYSIO. Well I have. And that's why I'm here.

KAT. Jesus told you to become a physiotherapist?

PHYSIO. Let's not give him too much credit. He told me
I should be helping people. I filled in the blanks.

KAT. And he still talks to you?

PHYSIO. Every day.

KAT. Well. That must be nice for you.

PHYSIO. You don't have to believe to understand what I'm
talking about.

He gives me a drive to become a better person. The bad news
for you is that drive also makes me a stubborn prick. A stubborn

prick who's not going to leave you alone until you do seven steps.

Five.

Six.

...

CATHERINE. I came before but you were asleep.

Met your mum. She's fun. Wanted to come. Say hello. Check you were alright.

It's good to see you out of bed though. You look better.

KAT. Who are you?

CATHERINE. You don't remember me?

Oh shit.

Sorry.

I came before but you were a bit. My name's Catherine. Nice to meet you.

I'm the one who saved you. Saved your life you know?

KAT. You.

CATHERINE. Me.

I'm the one who put you out. Didn't they tell you I was coming?

KAT. No.

CATHERINE. They said they were gonna tell you.

KAT. No.

CATHERINE. I ran over and put you out with my coat don't you remember? You were properly on fire and I ran over.

Look. You don't need to thank me. I'm just glad to see you're alright. Some people been saying I'm a hero or whatever but I just call that being a human being you know.

So how you doing? You doing okay? Your mum says you're doing loads better.

You got a nice room. Do you like it?

KAT. You stopped me?

CATHERINE. That's right.

KAT. Why?

CATHERINE. I'm sorry?

KAT. Why did you stop me?

CATHERINE. I don't understand.

KAT. You stopped me before anyone could see.

CATHERINE. Before –

Of course I did. You'd have died.

KAT. You had no right.

CATHERINE. I saved your life.

KAT. No fucking right.

CATHERINE. I'm sorry.

Are you angry?

KAT. Get out.

CATHERINE. Maybe I should go.

KAT. Get the fuck out of here!

CATHERINE. I'm. I'm going.

It was nice to meet you properly.

...

MUM *and* KAT.

KAT. Mum. I want you to do something for me.

MUM. Alright.

KAT. I want you to film me.

MUM. Film you? Doing what?

KAT. Show my bandages, my scars, and. I'll explain what
happened to the camera. Explain why I did it.

MUM. Oh Kat love.

   I know why you did it.

   I've read the letter you posted.

KAT. What.

MUM. It was waiting for me when I got home. That first terrible
   weekend when we weren't sure if you were ever going to
   wake up. I went home to pick up some things and it was
   sitting for me on my doormat.

   Can I ask you something?

   Why did you send it to me of all people?

KAT. I thought you'd understand.

MUM. Understand? I'm disgusted.

   I burnt that letter soon as I read it. Police were already asking
   questions. Tommy was distraught. Didn't want anyone else
   knowing about it if they didn't have to.

KAT. You should have told someone.

MUM. Then what? It makes the news and suddenly it all stops
   praise be our problems are solved because one woman's tried
   to top herself?

KAT. No. I don't know.

MUM. Look what you've done to yourself. And now you sit here
   and you say you want me to film you looking like –

KAT. I'm asking you –

MUM. I'm your mother. Imagine if it was you sat here and Jo in
   the bed burnt half to death.

   And Tommy.

   I've sat here. The whole time. Not been able to tell him he's
   been put through hell so you could do some sort of stunt or –

KAT. No. Not a stunt.

   I couldn't just sit around watching the news any more.

I had to do something Mum.

MUM. What's wrong with a fucking petition!

What about Jo? Did you even think about her?

KAT. Of course.

MUM. What she'd feel?

KAT. I did it for her.

MUM. Don't say that. Don't you say that.

KAT. It's her world too and people are suffering.

MUM. So what Kat? So what? They're strangers. She's your daughter.

I know I've not always been the best mother. But I would never have abandoned you. Never. Not for anything.

I would rather have seen a million strangers die screaming and hungry than have ever left you on your own. Have ever seen you get

Hurt.

And that doesn't make me a bad person. It makes me human. Look at your face. You're in agony.

And it didn't change a damn thing.

You want to change the world? You can do a hell of a lot more alive than dead my girl, don't you see? You could dedicate the next forty years of your life to changing things, if you wanted to. Now that's a lot harder. It'll take a lot more graft and it's a lot less showy. But it's a damn site more effective.

KAT. I had to Mum. I had to do this.

MUM. You didn't darling. And that's what breaks my heart.

KAT. I'll tell Tommy.

MUM. No.

KAT. He might understand.

MUM. No!

I want you to listen to me. Really listen to me.
The world is a terrible place. But guess what? It always has
been.
I've fought against things like this since before you were born.

But you know the thing about all those times? I wasn't by
myself. We fought together. And we lost. Over and over again
we lost. Oh boy. But we did it together.

No one ever changed the world alone. Not in this country.
We're not wired that way. You've got to believe in other people.

When someone does something like this we don't see a hero.
We see a lunatic. I'm sorry to say it but that's just the way it is.

KAT. If I don't tell anyone, it's all for nothing.

MUM. Oh Kat. It's already for nothing.

Tommy's coming back down next week. You know that boy is
never going to understand why you did this. And he shouldn't
have to.

Whatever drove you to do this, I want you to forget all about it.
You bury it down deep and you move on. You don't tell anyone.

Kat. Are you listening to me?

Whenever anyone asks you what happened you look them in
the eye and you lie. You lie with all your heart.

And you get out of here. Get better. Go back to living your
life. To raising that little girl.

KAT. Mum –

MUM. Family. Happiness. That's all that matters, really. We get a
little bit of happiness and then we die.

I love you so much.

My beautiful little girl.

KAT. You had no right.

MUM. I know I didn't.

But I'm your mum. So.

...

KAT *and the* PHYSIO.

PHYSIO. You ready? This is it. Fifteen steps from you to me.

KAT. Okay.

One step.

PHYSIO. Good. Two.

Two steps.

Three steps.

You're doing so well.

Four steps.

KAT. Ah fuck. Fucking fuck.

Five steps.

PHYSIO. Four. Five. Kat look at me. Focus on each movement.

Six steps.

That's it. You've got it in you Kat I know you do.

Seven steps.

Focus. Focus on all the things you're going to do when you get out of here. Let that drive you let that get you over the line.

Eight steps.

All the things you're going to do on the other side of those doors.

Nine steps. TOMMY *enters.*

TOMMY. Hiya Kat.

KAT. Tommy.

KAT *falters.*

TOMMY. Sorry. Keep going. Don't mind me.

PHYSIO. It's alright. We can stop.

KAT. No.

TOMMY. I'll stay out of the way.

PHYSIO. Do this you can do anything come on Kat. Six more.

Ten steps.

Come on. Take your time. Five left.

TOMMY. Keep going.

PHYSIO. Keep going Kat. Think of all the things you're going to be doing. Think of getting out of here and going home. Doing whatever you want.

Eleven steps.

Twelve.

Thirteen.

KAT *falters.*

KAT. I can't. No more.

It's too hard.

She breaks down.

TOMMY *rushes to catch her.*

TOMMY. Hey. Hey. It's alright. I've got you.

Two more.

He helps her take a step.

That's it.

Last one.

KAT. Tommy.

I'm sorry.

I'm so sorry.

Take me home.

...

THREE

FIFTEEN YEARS

TOMMY *and* KAT *arrive home.*
It's still difficult for KAT *to walk.*
TOMMY. Welcome home Kat.
KAT. Tommy.

   Let's shut out all the rest of it.

                          – The world gets worse. –

TOMMY *applies lotion to* KAT*'s burns.*
TOMMY. Every day that's what he said.

                          – The world gets worse. –

KAT. It hurts. Tommy.
TOMMY. I'm here.
KAT. Jo.
TOMMY. She's fine.

                          – The world gets worse. –

TOMMY. We don't have to see them if you don't –

                          – The world gets worse. –

KAT. I was cooking on the hob and the robe just went up.

FRIEND. Awful. Just awful.

KAT. Tommy saved me. Put me out. Didn't you?

TOMMY. Yeah.

– The world gets worse. –

KAT. Tommy. Wake up. I'm hot. I'm so –

TOMMY. Wait there –

KAT. Water I need –

– The world gets worse. –

TOMMY *applies lotion to* KAT*'s burns.*

KAT. Thank you. That feels –

– The world gets worse. –

TOMMY *and* KAT. Happy birthday dear Jo-o!

– The world gets worse. –

KAT. She doesn't want to be around me.

TOMMY. Hey. Of course she does.

KAT. The way she looks at me it's.

– The world gets worse. –

TOMMY. More money.

KAT. You always said –

TOMMY. I know. But it's more money. I might enjoy it.

– The world gets worse. –

TOMMY. You're shivering.

KAT. I'm fine.

TOMMY. I'm calling the doctor

KAT. I'm fine –

– The world gets worse. –

KAT. I was cooking. On the hob.

FRIEND 2. And Tommy –

TOMMY. I was in the other room and I ran in and put out the fire.

KAT. That's right.

– The world gets worse. –

KAT. I can't fight with you any more Mum.

MUM. Okay. Well I'm glad.

KAT. I just want to forget about all of it. Like you said. Is that okay?

MUM. Okay.

Just be happy love. That's all I want for you.

It's good to have you home.

– The world gets worse. –

KAT. How was it?

TOMMY. Good. Yeah. Far as first days go.

Bit boring but –

– The world gets worse. –

KAT. How was work?

TOMMY. How you feeling?

– The world gets worse. –

KAT. – you doing I told you not to come home.

TOMMY. I'm taking you to the hospital. No argu–

– The world gets worse. –

MUM. – being paranoid.

TOMMY. All due respect but she's not your daughter.

MUM. Tell him he's being paranoid –

KAT. I agree with –

– The world gets worse. –

FRIEND. – looking great. Isn't she?

TOMMY. She is.

FRIEND. You thought about what I said?

    Thank god you were there Tommy but the robe you were wearing should've been flame retardant.

    Get a lawyer. Go to the press.

TOMMY. You might be right.

FRIEND. What if it happens to someone else? A little kiddy whoosh.

    Flame retardant I'm –

– The world gets worse. –

COLLEAGUE. Kat. It's so good to see you.

    When I heard about what happened –

TOMMY. Her robe. On the hob.

COLLEAGUE. I heard. Awful. The last time I saw you it was on the train.

KAT. It happened a few days later.

COLLEAGUE. Right.

KAT. Tommy put me out.

TOMMY. I put her out.

COLLEAGUE. Is that right?
    Well. You're a bit of a hero aren't you. Thank god you were there.

    It's good to see you up and about.
    Are you thinking of coming back into work? We all miss you.

TOMMY. No.

KAT. Maybe.

COLLEAGUE. Right.

TOMMY. We're going to talk about it.

– The world gets worse. –

EVERYONE. Happy birthday dear Jo-o!

– The world gets worse. –

TOMMY. How was work?

KAT. Great. Really great.

TOMMY. You're not too –

– The world gets worse. –

MUM. – don't see what the big deal is.

KAT. I don't want the news on around her.

MUM. She doesn't understand.

KAT. The images. The things they –

– The world gets worse. –

COLLEAGUE. Isn't it awful? Those poor kids. I'm putting the kettle on you want something?

Makes you realise how lucky we are when you see footage like that. My son Peter –

– The world gets worse. –

KAT. I like working.

TOMMY. I just don't see why we should jeopardise your health when we don't need the money.

I'm doing great, everyone says so. Few more years like this and –

– The world gets worse. –

EVERYONE. Happy birthday dear Jo-o! Happy birthday to –

– The world gets worse. –

TOMMY. – in the other room watching telly and I heard this awful scream. I'll never forget that sound for as long as I live. Shouting my name weren't you? Of course instantly I knew what had happened don't know how sometimes you just know don't you? And I ran faster than I've ever run before and I just acted. You know? I grabbed this picnic blanket we had lying around from the weekend thank god it was there and I wrapped it round her until the flames were out and I just held her. Doctors said even a moment longer –

– The world gets worse. –

KAT. I'll get some ice.

TOMMY. Group of lads jumped him.

KAT. God.

TOMMY. Second time this month.

– The world gets worse. –

COLLEAGUE. Isn't it awful?

KAT. Yeah.

COLLEAGUE. I've given some money.

KAT. That's good.

COLLEAGUE. Well you've got to do something don't you?

KAT. Yeah. You do.

– The world gets worse. –

TOMMY *rubs lotion into* KAT*'s burns.*

– The world gets worse. –

TOMMY. – a takeaway? Or we could –

– The world gets worse. –

KAT. Hurts a bit when –

– The world gets worse. –

EVERYONE. Happy birthday dear Jo-o! Happy birthday to –

– The world gets worse. –

CATHERINE. You got somewhere we could talk?

KAT. How did you find me?

CATHERINE. Your name's on the company website. I've been waiting for hours.

You look well.

Can we go inside.

KAT. No.

CATHERINE. The last time I saw you –

KAT. I wasn't well.

CATHERINE. No that's okay.

> I needed to come to see you. To say sorry. I should never have put you out. It wasn't my place.

KAT. There's no need.

CATHERINE. Please.

> I can't stop. Picturing it. You on the grass. On fire. Orange on green.

> When I got home from the hospital that night I was so shook up. You were so angry and I couldn't work out why. Because it's a good thing what I did it's supposed to be a good thing. Saving someone's life.

> And I started to think. What it was for? Why was she doing it? I tried to imagine what it could have been. Looking for reasons. And the more I looked the more reasons I found.

> I can't stop watching the news. Reading everything I can.

> I need to know.

> What was it made you do it?

> Like, what was the reason?

> Was there a reason?

> What made you do it?

> Why did you do it Kat? Please. I just want to know. I could tell people maybe tell your story talk about what happened –

KAT. No. Nobody knows what happened that day. We've told everyone it was an accident. Please don't tell anyone.

> Forget about it. We have.

> I have to go.

CATHERINE. I'm sorry. I'm so sorry.

KAT. Don't ever contact me again.

– The world gets worse. –

EVERYONE. Happy birthday dear Jo-o!

– The world gets worse. –

FRIEND. This area's really gone downhill. We've started looking for a new place.

– The world gets worse. –

KAT. Jo! Dinner's ready!

– The world gets worse. –

EVERYONE. Happy birthday dear Jo-o! Happy birthday to you!

– The world gets worse. –

KAT. Jo! I think Santa's been…

– The world gets worse. –

EVERYONE. Happy birthday dear Jo-o!

– The world gets worse. –

KAT. Jo you get down here *right* now.

KAT *and* TOMMY. JO!

– The world gets worse. –

EVERYONE. Happy birthday dear –

– The world gets worse. –

KAT. Jo! Jo! Jo!

JO. Oh my god Mum? You okay?

KAT. I'm fine love. Just a bit. Give me a hand.

JO. Sit down.

    Shall I get you some water?

KAT. Thank you. Yes.

JO. I'm calling the doctor.

KAT. No. I'll be alright in a minute. Go and get on with your homework.

JO. Here.

KAT. Thank you. You're a good girl.

– The world gets worse. –

KAT. What did they say?

JO. Doesn't matter.

KAT. Were they making fun?

JO. They won't do it again.

– The world gets worse. –

MUM. Were you even listening to me?

KAT. Sorry Mum?

TOMMY. Sorry what?

MUM. You two. You're in your own –

– The world gets worse. –

FRIEND. I know they're all angry but the more they behave like
that the less people are going to listen to what they have to
say.

TOMMY. You're right. I was saying that exact same thing to –

– The world gets worse. –

EVERYONE. Happy birthday dear Jo-o!

– The world gets worse. –

MUM. – won't stop long I just wanted to see if you two were free
for the barbecue on Sunday.

KAT. You want Tommy to –

– The world gets worse. –

JO. This is really good Mum.

– The world gets worse. –

MUM. – snatched it right out of my hand the animal. Luckily there was a policeman nearby and they were able to catch the guy. Bag was long gone though.

TOMMY. This area. Haven't I been telling you?

– The world gets worse. –

TOMMY. I got it!

KAT. Oh Tommy that's wonderful! Congratulations!

TOMMY. This is gonna make such a difference to us, you watch.

– The world gets worse. –

JO. I hate you! It's not fair!

KAT. Well, the world's not fair.

– The world gets worse. –

TOMMY. They were out there again last night. We've got to move.

JO. I'm not moving.

TOMMY. We can afford better now.

KAT. You really think

JO. I'm not fucking moving.

KAT *and* TOMMY. Hey!

– The world gets worse. –

MUM. – it's very nice. Those exposed beams.

TOMMY. Gate out front. Guard's there twenty-four hours.

KAT. Closer to my new doctor.

TOMMY. See that alarm system? State of the art. Can be here in
fifteen minutes –

– The world gets worse. –

COLLEAGUE. Cut him down right in the street. Couldn't
believe it.

How's your new place?

– The world gets worse. –

EVERYONE. Happy birthday to you. Happy birthday to you.
Happy birthday dear Jo-o!

– The world gets worse. –

EVERYONE. Dear Jo-o!

– The world gets worse. –

EVERYONE. Dear Jo-o!

– The world gets worse. –

EVERYONE. Dear Jo-o!

– The world gets worse. –

KAT. Jo!

JO. I'm coming. Jesus.

– The world gets worse. –

KAT. You come straight home once it's finished. And don't talk
     to anyone. Let me give you some money for a taxi.

JO. Mum. I'll be fine.

KAT. Do not get the bus under any –

– The world gets worse. –

MUM. Hundreds of them. Suffocated.

KAT. Mum –

JO. I don't mind.

MUM. She needs to know.

KAT. I don't want her hearing those stories.

JO. I'm fine.

MUM. She's gonna find out about it one way or another.

TOMMY. We think it's best if –

– The world gets worse. –

EVERYONE. Happy birthday dear Jo-oooo!

– The world gets worse. –

TOMMY. Kettle's on.

– The world gets worse. –

KAT. – say that nobody above the thirteenth floor made it out.

TOMMY. I'm amazed it hasn't happened before.

– The world gets worse. –

TOMMY. – there's no excuse for that sort of behaviour. They look like a bunch of bloody animals. A lot of those windows belonged to local businesses. It's not the local businesses' fault. I'm sorry but –

– The world gets worse. –

EVERYONE. Happy birthday dear Jo-o! Happy birthday to you!

MUM. Give your nana a kiss then.

JO. Aw Nan. Get off.

– The world gets worse. –

KAT. Thank you for seeing me.

CATHERINE. Okay.

KAT. I wanted to talk to you.

I was horrible to you and I've regretted that ever since. I owe you everything Catherine. I never thanked you for that.

CATHERINE. No.

KAT. So thank you. Deeply.
   You don't look. Are you alright?

CATHERINE. Things are difficult.
   Everything is very difficult.

KAT. Do you need money?

CATHERINE. No. That's not.
   What are you doing here?

KAT. My daughter still doesn't know. She thinks I had an
   accident.

CATHERINE. You should tell her. She should know who her
   mum is.

KAT. I can't have her knowing. You understand?

CATHERINE. I should've let you burn.

KAT. Don't say that.

   I've seen my daughter grow up. Shared happiness with my
   husband. I'm living a good life and it's all thanks to you and
   I'm sorry I haven't said that before.

   Stopping me was the right thing to do.

CATHERINE. For you maybe. But for the rest of us?

   I live that day over and over. What you looked like. Smelt
   like. What made you do it.

   You saw all this coming and tried to do something about it.
   And I stopped you. And every day when I see whatever shitty
   thing has happened that morning I'm reminded of it.

   If I hadn't been there you might have changed everything.
   Stopped the rot before it set in.

KAT. I wasn't well.

CATHERINE. You don't actually believe that do you?

   You weren't mad. You were just ahead of the curve. You
   thought things were bad then. Look at them now. It's a wonder
   people aren't burning themselves every day.

Fifteen years on and everything's just got worse and worse and we still haven't hit the bottom. We just keep on burrowing into the shit.

But it's alright.

Because I'm –

– The world gets worse. –

KAT. This is our house.
    You can't just go letting homeless men in our kitchen.

JO. He was hungry. It's called being a human.

KAT. We could have been robbed. You could have been killed.

JO. Don't be so dramatic.

KAT. If you ever do something like that again.

JO. Just because you don't give a shit about the rest of the world doesn't mean the rest of us can't –

    KAT *slaps* JO.

KAT. I'm sorry.

    I'm so sorry. I shouldn't have done that.

JO. I thought I was doing a good thing.

KAT. I know.

    You were.

    Of course you were.

– The world gets worse. –

KAT. Thank you for coming, we really appreciate you all giving up your evenings.

I'll try and keep this short, because I know you all want pudding. God, I don't know where to start. Tommy always makes these things look easy.

There was a time when I never thought I'd see a day like today. If you told me I'd be standing here giving a toast to my husband I'd never have believed you in a million years. Any of you who knew Tommy at fifteen will understand.

When we first got together my mum would hate it. She'd be talking at us, asking us to do something. Take the bins out or do the washing up. And we just wouldn't hear her would we Mum? 'You're in your own little world you two.' That's what she always used to say. And she was right.

Because when I was with Tommy, nothing else mattered. And then we had Jo. And she mattered even more to us than we did to each other. If that was possible.

It hasn't always been easy. I haven't always been easy. But he has always taken care of me and he's given me a wonderful life and –

Happy anniversary.

Enjoy yourselves. And please, keep eating. There's far too much food.

To Tommy.

And to our little world.

– The world gets worse. –

MUM. The doctors have all been wonderful. Don't have to tell you about that.

I keep thinking, I wish I believed in an afterlife.

That'd be nice. That any day now it's going to be all blue sky and frozen margaritas. Instead of just…

KAT. Oh Mum.

MUM. Don't worry about me.

Maybe it's the right time to go eh? Everything's falling apart out there. My body sympathises.

Here.
I've got something for you.

MUM *takes out the letter* KAT *sent her.*

I know I said I destroyed it but. Well. There you go.

Passes it over.

KAT. You kept it? Why?

MUM. I'm sorry I ignored it. I'm sorry that I told you to lie about why you did. What you did. For so long.

I should never have done that.

KAT. No, Mum. You were right to. What good would it have done, anyone knowing?

MUM. I was so angry when I read that. I hated you for doing that to yourself. To your family. To me.

But despite that. Despite the anger and fear and sorrow that came into our lives that awful day. There was still a part of me that couldn't help feeling it was. Brave.

I mean it was fucking stupid. And selfish. So selfish. And I've wished every day from that one to this that you hadn't done it.

But. Brave.

I thought you should know that I always thought that.

KAT. Mum. Why did you keep this?

MUM. That's my daughter in those pages.

It's late.

I'm tired. Aren't you tired?

– The world gets worse. –

TOMMY. Hey. How you doing?

KAT. Okay.

TOMMY. What have you got there?

KAT. It's.

It's nothing. A letter I wrote to Mum, a long time ago.

I found it clearing out her bedroom.

TOMMY. I want you to know. Whatever you're feeling, whatever's going on in that head. You're not alone.

KAT. I know that.

TOMMY. And if you need to talk about your mum. Or. Anything.

I just want to make sure you're not thinking of. Or feeling –

KAT. Tommy. I'm okay.

TOMMY. Okay. Good.

What does the letter say?

KAT. I can't bring myself to read it yet.

Hey.

Come here.

Thank you. Thank you so much for everything.

– The world gets worse. –

KAT *alone. With the letter.*

She stares at it.

She screws it up without opening it.

A moment.

She changes her mind. Unfolds the screwed-up ball. Opens the letter.

She sits down and reads every word.

Finishes.

Something happens.

– The world gets worse. –

KAT *and* JO.

JO. Why didn't you tell me before?

KAT. I am so sorry.

JO. You should have told me.

KAT. I know.

   Are you okay?

JO. Dad knows?

KAT. He knows it wasn't an accident. Where it happened. He doesn't know why I.

JO. Why?

KAT. He never wanted me to tell him.

JO. No. Why did you do it?

   You wanted to kill yourself?

KAT. I don't know.

JO. Mum.

KAT. Yes. I did.

JO. Why?

   You were depressed?

KAT. No.

JO. Sick?

KAT. No. It's hard to explain.

JO. Try.

KAT. The world was getting worse and I wanted.

Needed. To.

Do something.
I wanted you to have a world that wasn't –

JO. I'm fine. The world is fine.

KAT. I know. I know you are.

Here.

She takes out the letter. Passes it to JO.

I wrote that to your nan on the day that I did it. Explaining.

Your dad's never seen it. Doesn't know it exists. I want you to read it.

You should know who your mum was. Is.

But when you read it I want you to remember.

Someone put out the fire. They saved my life. And not a day goes by when I'm not thankful that they did.

– The world gets worse. –

Parliament Square.

KAT *arrives.*

The bells chime.

It starts to rain. She sees CATHERINE. *She is holding a can of petrol.*

KAT. Catherine.

Why don't you put down the petrol?

CATHERINE. What are you doing here?

Didn't tell you to come. That's not why I told you.

KAT. I know that.

CATHERINE. You really shouldn't be here. I've made up my mind.

This is the spot right? Where you did it?

KAT. Close enough.

CATHERINE. You been back here since?

KAT. No.

CATHERINE. Must be strange.

CATHERINE *opens the petrol can.*

KAT. Wait –

Please.

CATHERINE *pours petrol all over herself. It stinks.*

CATHERINE. Stay back.

KAT. If you're doing this for me –

CATHERINE. I'm not.

KAT. Okay. Okay.

Why did you tell me?

CATHERINE. What?

KAT. You contacted me. You told me what you were going to do today.

CATHERINE. I wanted you to know.

KAT. You wanted me to stop you.

CATHERINE. No.

KAT. You wouldn't have told anyone if you didn't think they might stop you.

CATHERINE. I wanted you to know that what you did. All those years ago. It wasn't for nothing. That's all.

KAT. Of course it was. No one noticed.

CATHERINE. They'll notice this time.
Everyone's gonna be talking about it.

Look at all these people. Soon as I go up they'll be filming every second.

No one's gonna miss me doing this.

KAT. Even if that's true.
It won't change anything

You want to know what it feels like?

Agony. The worst pain. You can't imagine.

CATHERINE. That's not gonna work.

KAT. No one wants you to do this.

CATHERINE. Are you joking? Look around you. The world is crying out for someone to do this.

She raises the lighter.

KAT. Wait! Your family.

The people who care about you.

Think how they'll feel.

You don't –

CATHERINE. I don't.

KAT. You don't want to die.
Fight it.
It's not too late.

Put the lighter down. Go home. Have a bath. Eat a lasagne.

What I did.

I had my reasons.

I'd almost forgotten. But I had some really good reasons. And they haven't gone away.

But god. It wasn't worth it. There is no cause in the world that is worth doing this Catherine, I promise you.

CATHERINE. You don't really believe that, do you?

KAT. Look at me. Years I've lived in pain. Can't breathe properly. Can't move properly. Skin too tight. It wasn't worth it. I didn't change a thing that day.

CATHERINE. That's not true.

You changed me. Seeing you do that. It changed me.

KAT. One person.
One person by themselves is –

CATHERINE. Maybe that's all it takes.

Because I'm here now doing this and maybe me doing this is the thing that will change the world.

Or maybe I'll just change one of those people watching. Change that girl, that man, that woman and maybe they'll be the ones who change the world.

Maybe if I do this my face will go around my name will ring out and people will see that if they don't like what's going on they can get up out of their chairs and do something about it. They'll see me on fire and think to themselves 'if that woman can do that then I can do something to stop the rot. I can do something to stop the rot.'

Maybe a hundred more will set themselves on fire, person after person after person going up in flames until the world gets better until the world gets better. Imagine that.

Or maybe not.

But I've got to try, right? Because we've tried everything else.

KAT. You can still go home.

CATHERINE. Is that what you want?

KAT. Of course.

CATHERINE. If I do this. What you did. All those years of pain. It could mean something. Don't you want that?

It's alright Kat. I'm ready.

It's nice. How calm I feel.

She raises the lighter.

KAT. There's a lot of good in this world.

CATHERINE. You're right. There is.

That's why we've got to fight for it.

What do you think? Should I do it?

KAT. I

CATHERINE. Should I do it?

It's alright. Don't worry. I'm okay.

Just say yes.

Ages.

And then.

KAT. Yes.

CATHERINE *smiles as she flicks the lighter.*

She's on fire.

So bright.

KAT *shields her eyes from the light.*

1

2

3

4

5

6

7

8

9

10

11

12

13

14

15

– The world gets… –

LAVA

Acknowledgements

All the actors who helped workshop this play. Nottingham Playhouse for giving it a first home.

Tam for coming up with the title and putting up with mid-rewrite stresses.

Ted, Emma, Fred and Safiyya for bringing these characters so thrillingly into the world.

Nic Wass for her tireless dramaturgy and friendship across a long old process.

And Laura Ford and Angharad Jones, for taking a punt on me all those years ago and putting up with draft after draft after draft after draft with patience, insight and enthusiasm. We've made this together and I couldn't be more excited that it's finally a thing.

J.F.

Lava was first performed at Nottingham Playhouse on 15 June 2018, as a co-production between Fifth Word and Nottingham Playhouse. The cast was as follows:

JAMIE	Fred Fergus
RACH	Safiyya Ingar
VICKY	Emma Pallant
VIN	Ted Reilly

Director	Angharad Jones
Associate Director	Laura Ford
Designer	Amy Jane Cook
Lighting Designer	Alexandra Stafford
Sound Designer	Dan Balfour
Video Designer	Louise Rhoades-Brown
Dramaturg	Nic Wass
Casting Director	Christopher Worrall
Production Manager	Jill Robertshaw
Stage Manager	Kathryn Bainbridge-Wilson

It was revived at Soho Theatre, London, on 5 April 2022, with the following changes to cast and crew:

VICKY	Kacey Ainsworth
RACH	Bethany Antonia
JAMIE	Oli Higginson
VIN	Dan Parr

Co-Directors	Laura Ford and Angharad Jones
Production Manager	Jack Boissieux
Stage Manager	Eva Collins Alonso
Producer	Corinne Salisbury

Characters

RACH
VIN
VICKY
JAMIE

Note

Silence, for obvious reasons, plays a huge part in this play. I've suggested some places where silence might occur, but trust it throughout. The scenes between Vin and Vicky, in particular, should have painful silences running throughout them.

Dialogue in bold is sent from Vin's phone. It should never be spoken out loud by Vin, but should be able to be read or heard by the audience. I haven't included emoji, x's, etc., but feel free to add as you see fit.

An ellipsis (…) signifies a jump in time.

A line with no full stop at the end indicates an unfinished thought.

A line with a dash at the end indicates an interruption.

STAGE ONE: DENIAL

Time since impact: 15 days 7 hours 4 minutes 12 seconds.

VIN *and* RACH. RACH *is holding a candle.*

RACH   An asteroid

An actual fucking

Asteroid.

I can't be the only one who finds it a bit much.

Silence.

Like

I sort of

Wanna refuse

You know?

Refuse to be part of a world where something that ridiculous can happen.

Silence.

Like, if the news were a TV show, then the moment a little asteroid hit North London and killed twelve thousand people I'd stop watching. I'd be like, 'No thank you, they've gone way too far here.'

You know what I mean? They're taking the mick.

Silence.

What did you think of the vigil? Bit much, weren't it?
My mum's mate. Lucy.
She died.
She lives in London and she was on her way home when it hit.

Silence.

Hence the candle.

She gestures to the candle.

Silence.

Oh my god, you'll love this. I was doing a shift with Becca on Monday

She keeps going round to everyone saying how she almost died

So I was like, 'How did you almost die Becca?'

And she was like, 'I was sposed to go visit my cousin in London that weekend. But I didn't.'
And so I was like, 'So your cousin lives near the impact zone?'
And she was like, 'Not really, why?'

Her cousin lives in Croydon. That's not even London.

Silence.

Where you been hiding Vin?

You just disappeared on me. Came into work and there was a Vin-shaped hole where you used to be.

I text you. I know you've seen them. Did I do something to

How you been anyway? You been up to much?

Brief silence.

Right. You know it's pretty rude not to answer people in the same way it's pretty rude disappearing on your mates without a word. I'm just saying.

VIN *doesn't say anything.*

I get it.

Nice talking to you.

Fucking rude.

...

RACH   Sorry I called you rude.

I went into work and I said I saw Vin he's rude and Supervisor Ian was like oh yeah he just don't talk any

more. And I was like what d'you mean he don't talk
any more and he was like he just stopped talking which
was a bit of a problem it being a call centre and all.

That true then?

That's weird innit mate?

Is it like a brain thing?

My grandad had that.
After his stroke.

'Cept his was a bit different
Like
He could talk right
But he could only say one word which was

'Judy'

You know, like the name? I mean, he'd use it for
everything.

We'd be like
You hungry Grandad?
And he'd say 'Judy.'
You warm enough?
'Judy!'

And we were like, 'Who the fuck is Judy?' you know,
because my nan's name's not Judy my nan's name's
Jane.
And Nan was all like, 'Oh he probably picked it up off
the telly.'
But then

At his funeral
This woman shows up
Looking all
You know
Really glam right
And she don't say nothing
But she leaves some flowers
And on the card it says
'Forever yours. Judy.'

So what d'you think that was all about then?!

Can you write things down? Or your phone. You could text? You can't use your phone? I'm sorry mate. That is rough.

People don't just stop talking for no reason. Do they?

You want me to leave you alone?

Alright then I'll leave you alone.

...

RACH *and* VIN. VIN*'s front door.*

RACH   I've decided.

I'm not going to leave you alone. Ian gave me your address which is probably illegal but then we both know he's not great at his job is he?

Look how annoyed he is! He won't even look at me.

Vin!
Oi Vin!

VIN *refuses to look at her.*

Vin!
Vin!
Vin!
Vin!
Vin!
Vin!
Vin!
Vin!

I'm just gonna keep saying your name until you look at me.

Vincent!
Vinno!
Vin!
Vin!
Vinny!
Vin.
Vin

Vin.
Vin.
Vin.
Vin.
Vin.
Vin.
Viiiiiiiiiiiiiiiiiiiiiiiiiiiiiiiiiiiiiiiiiiiiiiiiiiiiiiiiiiiiiiiiiiiiiiiiiiiiiii
iiiiiiiiiiiiiiiiiiiiiiiiiiiiiiiiiiiiiiii

She takes a breath.

Iiiiiiiiiiiiiiiiiiiiiiiiiiiiiiiiiiiiiiiiiiiiiiiiiiiiiiiiiiiiiiiiiiiiiiiiiiiiiii
iiiiiiiiiiiiiiiiiiiiiiiiiiiiiiiiiiiiiiiiiin.

He looks at her. She grins.

Hiya.

Not being able to talk. Fucking hell.
I wouldn't last an hour. Having all that inside of me
and no place to put it I'd worry I'd explode.
At work. They said you stopped talking round the
same time as the asteroid. Same day, they thought.
That true?

VICKY   (*From inside the house.*)
Vin?! Who's that?

RACH   That your mum?

You gonna invite me in?

Okay.

Look how 'bout this. Here's my address.
Knock round any time.

...

VIN *and* VICKY. VIN's *house.*

VICKY   Hiya love.

Who was at the door?

A friend?

Anyone I know?

Okay.

Still not

That's fine.

There's food if you're

Oh! I forgot to say, that cat was back. I was stood in the garden and there he was, acting like he was the little King of Everything, oh you shoulda seen him.

Seems very friendly. For a cat, anyway.

I don't think he's got an owner, he's got no, whatsit, collar and he doesn't seem very well you know, cared for, his fur's sorta mangy, mind you that's just how some of them look isn't it?

I've given him some food either way, I thought what's the harm, you know, a bit of food, I picked up some, whatsit, cat biscuits from the Co-op I thought maybe I'll keep leaving some out for him, see if he comes back, what d'you think?

Might be nice. Having him in the house? Eh?

Seems friendly.

I wondered.

Fish and chips.
We haven't done that since

We could watch a film together.

Or football. Is there any good football on?

A film then.

Doesn't have to be fish and chips.

A curry?
Thai?
Chinese?
Pizza?
Barbecue?
Vietnamese?

Or I could cook something.

Or we could go out for dinner.

Or we could
We could

Okay.

I'll choose then, shall I?

...

VIN *is outside* RACH*'s house.*

RACH   Vin.

You're at my house.

Hello.

You want to come in? You can come in but just so you
know it's a bit weird in there at the moment. We just
got back from Lucy's funeral and Mum's a bit

They've only just been able to have it. Her son Jamie.
He gave this amazing speech and everyone was a wreck.

Kinda strange knowing someone who was in it.
You know what I mean?

D'you know what? It's pretty depressing in there.
D'you wanna go somewhere and get some cans?

...

They drink cans overlooking the town.

RACH   There's something going on round here.

Things keep disappearing.

Have you noticed? Like someone's stealing them.

It started small. Little things so you wouldn't.
The post box by my house. Gone. A lamp post on
Tudor Road I swear I passed it every day and then one
day. Gone.

Then it was The Black Sheep. Loved that pub. Then the swimming pool just vanished and nobody talked about it. A whole fucking swimming pool. Water and everything. And it wasn't like it was demolished there'd be bricks and stuff. It was just like one day it was there and the next day it wasn't. Same thing happened to the library. Remember the old library?

VIN *shakes his head.*

No course you don't. No one does. That's part of it you see. These things vanish and then everyone acts like they were never there to begin with.

Not me though. I pay attention. I'm on to them. The thieves. Maybe it's aliens. Eh? Don't look at me like that. If an asteroid's acceptable then I don't see how aliens is pushing things too far.

Or maybe we're like in a simulation or a game and we're just being deleted pixel by pixel. There's got to be an explanation.

Maybe that's where your voice has gone. Same place as the swimming pool.

Let's hope not. Eh?

VIN *nods.*

I wondered if you wanted if you fancied that maybe we could work it out together. I could help you try and get it back. If you wanted.

Because. Well. You know, and I don't know if this makes any, but I thought I'd

Cos when you did used to speak at work or in the pub I always kinda liked the things you had to say.

And I miss hearing them, if I'm honest.

VIN *smiles.*

Eurgh, that was fucking embarrassing.

What is it about having to fill a silence that makes some people say

Like
The most embarrassing shit

Forget I ever

I want to help
Is what I'm trying to say.

I'm here if you need me.

Silence.

I don't know if I should

You see Supervisor Ian at work told me something.

He told me something and I wasn't sure if I should say
but.

He told me he heard that your dad died in London.

Is that true?

He told me your dad died and you haven't been able to
talk to anyone since.

Because that makes sense.

That makes sense I bet.

A moment.

VIN *nods.*

Oh mate.

I am so sorry.

...

VIN *and* VICKY. VIN*'s house.*

VICKY   He's gonna be okay.

That's what the vet said.

Just a bit undernourished.

Wasn't sure if that was the right thing to
Taking him to the vet's.

I mean he might have another owner but he seemed
a bit

He's made himself at home here so it's only fair we
take care of him. Don't you think?

As I was leaving I bumped into Will Paxton with his
Labrador. He likes you.

Said that job offer's still going if you want it. So that's
good isn't it?

What do you think?

Might be good for you. Get out of the house. Get you
off that sofa.

Silence.

Bit of exercise. Lots of lads your age working on his
site he says. So that might be

But you know a job like that. You can't do the silent
act. Health and safety. Not safe for the other lads. You
know?

So I thought maybe together we could look at some
things. Websites or. Get you talking again. Because
I know things have been a bit rough, and we've all got
our own ways of

But we've got to get on with it, haven't we?
That's all we can do. Really.

So I'll tell him yes?

Yes?

Okay.

Good.

Good lad.

Vin's alright I told him. My Vin's doing alright.

What shall we call him then?

The cat.

Any suggestions?

...

Outside RACH*'s house.*

RACH   Vin.

You're at my house again. We really need to sort out a system.

I had fun the other night.

Listen there's something I should

JAMIE *enters from the house.*

JAMIE   Rach?
You ready?

RACH   Oh.

Vin this is Jamie. He's staying with us.

JAMIE   Hey man.

RACH   Just for a little while.

JAMIE   How's it going?

RACH   Vin can't talk.

JAMIE   What like, at all?
HOW'S IT GOING MATE?

RACH   You don't need to shout.

JAMIE   Right.

RACH   Jamie's from London. He was in the

JAMIE   Impact Event.

RACH   You remember I told you about his mum.

JAMIE   She died. Yeah.

RACH   His house might have structural damage so he's gonna stay with us until it's sorted.

Is it alright if I tell him. Vin?

RACH   Vin's dad died in London too.

JAMIE   You're kidding?

JAMIE *hugs* VIN *unexpectedly and fervently.*

It is so nice to meet you mate.

RACH   I was gonna take Jamie to The Talbot. For a pint.

Why don't you come?

STAGE TWO: ANGER

Residents displaced: 132,157.

VIN, RACH *and* JAMIE. *The pub.*

JAMIE   Are you furious Vin?

         I'm still fucking furious.

         It's a dereliction of duty.

RACH   You said.

JAMIE   A dereliction of duty.
         Someone must have seen it coming.
         I don't care what they say. The billions they spend
         on satellites.
         Weather technology.
         And NASA. What were they doing? Having a fag?

RACH   It does seem a bit mad.

JAMIE   My dad thinks we should sue them.

RACH   Who / NASA?

JAMIE   She died in my arms Vin, did you tell him Rach?

RACH   No I –

JAMIE   One minute she's there and the next

RACH   You don't have to talk about it if you don't feel –

JAMIE   No it's fine.
         Honestly.
         It helps actually.
         The thing I can't get over. It's the randomness.

         The chances of it hitting Earth in the infinity of space.
         The chances of it hitting London.

         And then the chances that my mum would be cycling
         through at that exact moment. That exact moment, not
         five minutes before, or five minutes after.

         What about your dad? Did he live round there?

VIN *shakes his head.*

RACH   Vin's dad's from here.

JAMIE   So he was just visiting?

VIN *nods his head.*

Oh mate. At least my mum, you know, she passed through there every day.

My house is only just outside the impact zone. We still can't go back. Structural damage.

RACH   I told him.

JAMIE   They rehoused us in this shitty B&B in Basingstoke, you ever been to Basingstoke?

VIN *shakes his head.*

Don't bother.

RACH   Why didn't your dad come too?

JAMIE   It is so funny being back round here. It's like stepping back in time.

Hasn't changed since I was a kid.
Used to come here all the time Vin.

RACH   We're sort of like cousins.

JAMIE   I'd say more like mates. When we were kids.
How do you two

RACH   We worked together.
Call centre.

JAMIE   Oh that is so interesting.

RACH   Okay.

JAMIE   Sometimes
And you'll love this
Sometimes when call centres ring me up I pretend that I'm really interested I sort of string them along for ages and pretend I'm going to give loads of money and then right at the last minute I'll do like a silly voice or something and tell them it was all a wind-up.

RACH   Yeah.
        We love it when people do that.

JAMIE   Can I ask
        I don't want to sound rude but
        How can you work in a call centre when you can't,
        you know...

RACH   Vin doesn't work there any more. He used to speak.

        It's only been since his dad

JAMIE   Oh mate.
        You know that makes perfect sense to me. Going
        through something like this. It takes a physical toll.

        Was he killed by the initial impact? Or in the
        aftermath?

        Do you know exactly where he was?

RACH   Maybe we should talk about something else.

JAMIE   Did you have trouble organising the funeral?
        We had terrible trouble. The backlog.

RACH   You even had a funeral yet?

        VIN *shakes his head.*

JAMIE   Ours took forever to get it sorted.
        Great day though
        Right Rach?
        Like, sad, but.
        A celebration as well.

        We did all these things
        Like we got my mate to DJ
        And we asked everyone to wear like their craziest
        colours.

        One of my uncles insisted on wearing black.
        And I was like
        Come on man
        It's not what she would've wanted.

RACH   I thought your speech was nice.

JAMIE   Thank you. That is so

It was like
The hardest thing I've ever had to write
But also
In a way
The easiest.

I'd be happy for you to read it, Vin. You know, if you
thought it might help.

A moment. VIN *nods.*

You know what. I've got a copy somewhere –

RACH   You don't have to

JAMIE   I don't mind.

He looks for the speech on his phone.

There you are.

You don't have to read it now.

Well you can read it now if you want to I don't mind.

VIN *starts to read the speech.*

JAMIE *watches him. It takes a while. Eventually* VIN
passes back the phone.

There's actually another page if you want to

JAMIE *flicks the page over.*

VIN *carries on reading.*

VIN *'s finished the speech. Hands back the phone.*

JAMIE   Thanks man.
Hope that was helpful.

A moment. VIN *nods.*

...

VIN *and* RACH.

RACH   I'm sorry about him.

I know he can be a bit

Mum and Dad didn't tell me he was coming. He just showed up and they were like Jamie's coming to stay with us for a while be nice to him he's been through a lot.

Still. Might be nice? Having someone else who knows what you're going through?

Suddenly VIN *texts her. We can see what he says.*

VIN   **Rach.**

RACH   Oh my god. You text me.

VIN   **Yeah.**

RACH   You did it again!

How long have you been able to text me?

That's great Vin. That's got to be a step in the right direction don't you think?

VIN   **I need to tell you**

RACH   Okay.

VIN   **There's been a mix-up**

RACH   What about?

VIN   **Dad didn't die in London.**

RACH   What.
        What are you talking about?

VIN   **Work assumed**

RACH   Why would you let me think that?

VIN   **I'm sorry. I came round to tell you the truth. But Jamie**

RACH   What truth?

        Whatever's going on. You can tell me.

VIN   **He didn't die in London. He died the same day.**

...

VIN, RACH *and* JAMIE.

JAMIE   The same day?

RACH   Vin found him on the kitchen floor.

JAMIE   Oh mate. You could've told me.

RACH   He felt embarrassed.

JAMIE   Well.
    He shouldn't. Grief's grief, you know.
    It doesn't matter if it's from an asteroid or a car
    accident or what did you say?

RACH   A heart attack.

JAMIE   It all counts.

    If anything it's easier for me knowing twelve thousand
    other families are going through the same thing, you
    know what I mean?

RACH   He's sorry he misled you.

JAMIE   No apology necessary.

    And my offer still stands. If ever you want someone to
    talk to.

    We could go for a pint or a walk?

RACH   What do you think Vin?

JAMIE   Another time maybe.

    I'll stop pestering you.

    How's your mum coping with things?

...

VIN *and* VICKY. VIN*'s house.*

VICKY   Gus.

That's the name I've chosen.

Short for Augustus.
What do you think?
Do you think he looks like a Gus?

I do.

Gus.

Gus.

I like it.

So come on then. How's the new job going?
Will treating you alright? Yeah.

That's so good Vin. That's so good. I mean it.

I'm really proud of you.
Working.
I know it must be hard.

Sarah said she saw you.
In the pub. With a girl. Was it that one that came to the house?

I think that's. Great.

Really.

I think it's wonderful that you feel comfortable
enough to.

That there's someone you can.

I'd love to meet her.

Why don't you bring her round, eh?

Or not.

Up to you.

...

VIN *and* RACH.

RACH   Jamie's mum's gonna have her name on a wall.
        That's mad innit?

        I gotta ask

VIN   **What?**

RACH   Does it piss you off that your dad died the same day as
        like, the maddest natural disaster in our lifetime?

        I mean it's pretty unlucky.

VIN   **come on.**

        don't ask me that.

RACH   Why not?

        Now you can text me I can finally ask you questions
        that don't end in yes or no

And what, you think I'm gonna waste that asking what you had for breakfast or whether or not you got off with Maria at the staff party which everyone knows you did by the way –

He smiles. Shrugs.

Does it piss you off that he died the same day?

You can be honest.
It'd piss me off.

VIN   **Honestly?**

A moment. Then –

Yeah
It's fuckin annoying

RACH   I knew it. It makes you feel –

VIN   **Insignificant.**
Invisible.

like why that day

RACH   Right?

VIN   **Why THAT EXACT FUCKIN DAY**
FUCKSAKE

A moment.

Sometimes
I'm reading about it
and I'm like
fuck them
And their memorials

A moment.

And then
You know
I feel like a dick.

RACH   No.
That's normal.

I'd feel the same.
Honest.

The not talking. Is it like you don't want to talk, so
you don't? Or you try and talk but you can't?
I've heard you talk before. You were pretty good at it.

VIN   **The words are in there.**
        But it's like they're in a lift
        And it gets stuck halfway up

RACH   Right. That makes sense.

VIN   **Speaking now would feel**

        Impossible.

RACH   Do you think you'll ever be able to talk to anyone?

VIN   **To anyone?**

RACH   To me.

        Silence.

        Don't hate me.

        But I've been looking it up. And there are things you
        can do. To help.

        Like there's an exercise where you hum quietly to
        yourself every morning. Get used to the feeling of
        your voice in your throat again. Just a little
        mmmmmmmmmm.

        You know. Maybe you could start doi–

        VIN *shakes his head.*

        I just thought it might help. Or there's this other article
        I read –

        What's the matter?

VIN   **I don't need you to help me.**

RACH   Okay.

        Well. Okay.

VIN   **I didn't btw**

RACH   Didn't what?

VIN   **Get off with Maria.**

                              ...

VIN *and* VICKY. VIN*'s house.*

VICKY   Good day at work love?

         Will treating you alright?

         VIN *nods.*

         That's good. That's really good.
         And the other lads. Been making some friends?

         VIN *shrugs.*

         Only I saw Will and he says you never came in.
         Says he hasn't seen you down at the site once.

         Where have you been going?

         Come back here. Come back.

         I just want to know what you've been doing. Because
         my mind's been racing love, it has. Because as far as
         I'm concerned you've been leaving this house and
         going to work and in actuality you've been going off
         to god knows where.

         Are you in trouble? Is there something you need to
         tell me?

         He shakes his head.

         God. Sometimes you can be so

         Look, Vincent. If you don't want to work there just say.
         It was just a suggestion. You don't have to lie to me.

         I'm only trying to help. I just thought that it might

         Because sitting round here all day isn't gonna make
         you feel any better is it? Is it?

'No Mum it isn't.' 'Sorry Mum thanks for trying.'

I mean, you're not a kid any more, you've got to try something? Surely? Snap yourself out of it somehow?

No.

Okay.

Let's just

...

VIN *and* RACH. RACH*'s bedroom.*

RACH   There's nothing there now, I'm telling you. A third of Tunnel Road just gone. I used to walk that way to work, it's fucking annoying.
It goes up to number 32 and then it just stops. I asked this old guy who lived there what happened to the other houses and he looked at me like I was mad and just said, 'It always stopped at number 32.' I was like, are you on a wind-up! The swimming pool was bad enough. But this!

What was his name. Your dad. You've never told me?

VIN   **Horatio**

RACH   Really?

VIN   **No.**

RACH   Dickhead.

VIN   **Phil.**

RACH   Phil.

The other day, when I asked, you said you hadn't had his funeral yet.

VIN   **Mum didn't want one.**

RACH   She didn't want one?

VIN   **Didn't see the point.**

             Brief silence.

RACH   What did he do, your dad?

VIN   **Electrician.**

RACH   Was he any good?

VIN   **He was**
             Fucking awful

RACH   Come on.

VIN   **Seriously. The worst.**

             When I was four
             He rewired my bedside lamp.
             Electrocuted me.

RACH   No.

VIN   **Flew across the room.**
             See that.

             He shows her a burn.

             Man was a liability.

RACH   You must miss him.

             Silence.

             How's your mum?

             She still pissed off about the job?

VIN   **I tried.**
             Went down there.
             But couldn't.

RACH   You gonna try again?

VIN   **No point.**

RACH   Maybe there's a job we can think of where being
             silent's a good thing.

             Like a guard at Buckingham Palace. Or a librarian.

You'd make a good accomplice. You know. To a
crime. You could be like the driver or something and
when the police interrogate you asking like where are
they where are your partners you'll be like

Ooh. You could be a lip-sync artist?

Don't look at me like that.

It's a thing. I'll show you a clip

...

RACH *is lip syncing to a famous song. She is quite good.*
VIN *starts to enjoy it.*

She encourages him to join in. He refuses.

*She gets to the climax of the song. They dance and it is silly.
There's a moment. They stare at each other.*

Brief silence.

RACH   Vin.

        Am.
        Am I the only person you can text?

VIN   **Course**

RACH   'Course'. I don't know do I.

        Just me. No one else?

        VIN *shakes head.*

        Why?

        What's special about me, I mean?

        Must be something.

        A moment between them.

        They almost kiss.

        VIN *moves away.*

        Sorry.

        No.

I'm a

Sorry. I shouldn't have done that. I thought maybe.

I don't know what I thought.

STAGE THREE: BARGAINING

Total raised for survivors: £2,751,570.

VIN*'s house.*

VICKY   I think I'm going a bit mad.

        This morning the neighbour you know the bin Nazi she caught me out on the street having a full-blown conversation with the cat. In my nightie.

        He was out there and it was raining and I was worried about him being near the road. And I kept saying

        'Gus if you come in I'll give you some smoked salmon.' 'Gus if you come in I'll let you sleep on the bed tonight.'

        And the neighbour she looked at me like 'what is that madwoman doing?' And so I waved at her. But she didn't wave back.

        So that's the last time I can show my face out the front door, eh?

        How was last night then? You have a good time?

        Can't wait to meet her. Your mysterious pub friend.

        Do you
        Do you talk to her Vin? You know. Out loud.

        A moment.

        VIN *shakes his head.*

        Okay.

        So there really isn't anyone who you

He shakes his head.

Well. Just so I. Just so I know.

...

VIN *and* RACH.

RACH   The other night.

VIN   **There's something
       I should say.**

RACH   No
       You don't have to.
       I feel awful.
       Feel like a right dickhead

VIN   **No.**

RACH   There's you
       And you're grieving
       You're in grief
       And you're telling me all this stuff about your grief
       and your dad and
       And there's me
       And I'm just just launching myself at you like a
       I don't know
       A sex pest or
       A

       And
       And now you're laughing.
       You're laughing at me. That's nice. That's making me
       feel less embarrassed thanks.

VIN   **It's alright.**

RACH   No.
       It was stupid.
       I'm sorry.

       You don't have to worry.
       It won't happen again.

       Brief silence.

VIN   **How's Jamie?**

RACH   I thought he'd've gone home by now. I don't even
         know what he's still doing here.
         His dad's in Basingstoke.

         Mum's still in overdrive. Fresh towels. Clean sheets.
         Orange juice.

         He's starting to annoy me a bit. If I'm honest.

         Is that bad?

         I know he's been through a lot but.

         He drops references to it all the time.

         Like, all the time.

         I'll be like. 'Pass the butter.' And then he goes all sad
         and is like 'Oh. My mum used to love butter.'

         I'm gonna take him to the pub.

         Mum's making me.

         You wanna come?

         Please come.

                        …

VIN, RACH *and* JAMIE. *The pub.*

JAMIE   My mum would've loved this pub.
         She'd have been like, this pub. It's got such a weird
         crowd. I love it.

RACH   It's not that weird.

JAMIE   It is.
         Come on.
         In a good way. Don't you think?

         Like, who's that guy in the old England shirt who's
         talking to himself outside?

RACH   David Beckham?
         That's what we call him.

JAMIE   Hilarious. He is mad.

RACH   Yeah.

JAMIE   Like an actual madman.

RACH   Story goes he came home from watching England Argentina in the pub to find out his whole family had died in a fire. Wife. Two little girls. He hasn't taken off the shirt since.

Could be bollocks.

JAMIE   Right.

Silence.

You know when I told the barman I was a London survivor he gave me a free shot. I get that sort of reaction all the time.

I've just felt so welcome since I got here.

I hope I haven't been too annoying.
Just this random guy from your childhood showing up at your house uninvited and bumming everyone out by mentioning his dead mum all the time.

RACH   Why would you think that?

JAMIE   Because I really appreciate it. I do.

It's just what I need being round here.

You know. There's nothing going on.

In a good way.

I was gonna ask.
Since I'm staying.

Do you think there are any jobs going?

At the call centre?

RACH   You wanna work with me? Why?

JAMIE   Might as well keep myself busy.

RACH   You won't enjoy it.

JAMIE   Meet some new people.

RACH   Vin tell him he won't enjoy it.

JAMIE   It can't be that bad.

RACH   It is.

JAMIE   Then why would anyone work there?

RACH   Because they need money.

Silence.

It's not forever

JAMIE   No

RACH   I got a plan.

JAMIE   That's great.

RACH   Save enough.
Move out.
Start my own business

JAMIE   What business?

RACH   Don't matter.
So long as it does well. Which it will.

And then once that's up and running and everyone
knows who I am

You'll laugh.

JAMIE   I won't.
I promise.

RACH   I'm gonna run for Mayor.

JAMIE   What like with the gold chains?

RACH   I told you not to laugh.

JAMIE   I'm not. Sorry.

RACH   This town is the best.
It is.
It's fucking amazing.
Just needs a bit of fixing.

Most at my college would give me that same look.
Couldn't wait to get away.
Even those that knew they weren't going anywhere
spent their whole time putting it down.

I'm like well do something about it. Make it better.
Don't just fuck off and leave it to die.

So that's my plan. Start a shit-hot local business.
Run for Mayor. Sort shit out.

JAMIE   Well. I'd vote for you.

RACH   Don't take the piss.

JAMIE   I'm serious.
I think that's great. I think you'd be great.

Don't you Vin?

VIN *nods*.

RACH   I can ask.
At work.
I'm sure they'll take you.
But

Trust me. You'll hate it.

...

JAMIE   I love it!
What a job. Seriously.

At first I was like, this is really boring all you do is sit
there and call people.
And then I was like, wow. This is really cool. All you
do is sit there and call people. Talk to them, you know.
Conversations.

I've had so many interesting conversations today you
know people can be so fascinating if you let them.
There was this one lady who was eighty-four and she
told me her life story.

RACH   They'll do that.
You've got to be firm.

JAMIE   No no it was amazing.

She told me the most impossible thing.

She told me that she grew up during the Hungarian
revolution.

And when she was twenty-one she fell in love
With a man called Victor.
But one day, about a week before her wedding, Victor
was shot dead. Right in front of her.

Her heart was broken. She swore off romance forever.
Cut to, she's in her fifties and she's still all alone
And she's walking her dog in the park when she
bumps into this man and she looks up and she realises.
It's him. It's Victor.

RACH   Shut up.

JAMIE   Her great love.
In the flesh. Only older.
And of course she thinks she's seen a ghost
That he's come back to haunt her
Until she remembers that Victor had a

Twin brother

Who she'd never met.

RACH   Fuck off!

You're joking.

JAMIE   I know right? So they reconnected and suddenly she
found herself falling in love with the brother and
they've been together thirty-two years.

What are the chances of that?

Isn't that like fucking romantic?

RACH   Vin he's such a show-off.
He got like ten donations on his first day.

JAMIE   Is that good? I didn't even notice.

Thanks so much for getting me in.

RACH   No worries.

It was actually nice having someone to talk to.

JAMIE *winces.*

Your thumb playing up?

JAMIE   It's no big deal.

RACH   He dislocated it Vin.

JAMIE   I dislocated it Vin.

RACH   It was during the

JAMIE   During the impact yeah that's right.

We were running for our lives and this girl she tripped and I hauled her up and as I did

Didn't want to leave anyone behind you know.

It was fine. Just meant I couldn't practice guitar for a few weeks, that's all.

RACH   My dad's got a guitar.
I'm sure he'd let you have a go.

JAMIE   Oh god no, I'm too shy.

...

RACH *'s house.* JAMIE *is holding a guitar.*

JAMIE   So I've been playing for a little while.
Just sort of messing about.

He plays a supercool riff.

You know. Just sort of.

He plays another supercool riff. Maybe sings a note.

So yeah.
I'm just sort of –

Without missing a beat he launches into a sad, beautiful, sincere, slightly irritating song. He sings every verse and every chorus. Every time VIN *thinks he's going to stop he keeps going, seemingly forever. Eventually, after an eternity, the song finishes.* RACH *claps.* VIN *does one or two claps.*

RACH   That was.
Yeah.

JAMIE   Thanks yeah. I played it at Mum's funeral. Every time
          I sing it it's like she's singing it with me.

          Silence.

          Did your dad have a favourite song Vin?

          VIN *shakes his head.*

          There's also this one.

          *He starts the first few bars of another very sincere,
          probably irritating song.*

                              ...

VIN *and* VICKY. VIN*'s house.*

VICKY *about to leave.* VIN *on the couch.*

VICKY   Okay then.

          I'm off out.

          There's a pizza in the fridge and I've already given
          Gus his food so don't give him any more you know
          what he's like.

          What you doing with yourself?

          You seeing your mates tonight?

          He shrugs.

          Okay.

          Can I ask

          I've seen, Vin.

          I've

          I've noticed that

          You text her. A lot.

          You feel alright texting her?

          A moment. VIN *nods.*

          Well.
          That's good, isn't it?

That's great.

That's a good step, eh?

I wonder I've been wondering

maybe.

Maybe you could try texting

me?

VIN *freezes*.

It could be good for us. A good step for us. You could start telling me what you want. Answering my questions. We could text. Or I could talk and you could text.

What do you say? Shall we give it a go?

VIN *shakes his head*.

No.

Okay.

Am I

Am I doing something wrong, love? Because if I am just tell me and I'll try and stop I will

VIN *shakes his head.*

Okay. Well. Let me know.

I won't be late.

...

VIN *and* RACH.

RACH   I'm getting used to having him around.

It's nice having a friend at work again.

Everyone fucking loves him. It's annoying.

The other day I came into the break room and Jamie was sat there with everyone looking at him. Turns out he's been telling the story of how his mum died because everyone had this like devastated look on their faces.

Even Supervisor Ian looked like he'd been crying. I know.

Still think it's weird that Jamie seems so sort of. Fine. You know what I mean? After everything he's been through.

I mean the things he must have seen that day.

And his mum. God knows what he's feeling.

VIN *nods.*

Idiot. Course you know.

VIN   **It's okay.**

RACH   No. Vin. I'm sorry.

          I thought
          And this is just an idea
          But
          We could have like a funeral for your dad.
          Or not a proper funeral.
          It wouldn't have to be formal or anything.
          We could go to the park.
          Light a fire.
          Drink some cans.
          Just something to mark his life.
          You know?
          Maybe that's
          It might be the reason that you can't
          That you're finding it hard to talk about him.

          Because if you've had no release

VIN   **Nah.**

          Thanks.

RACH   Okay.

          It was just a suggestion.

Well

What about talking to Jamie?

He offered

And he's obviously dealing with losing his mum

Differently. To you.

He might be able to give you some advice?

It's worth a try isn't it?

For me?

...

JAMIE *and* VIN.

JAMIE   Mate.

I am so glad you wanted to do this.

Seriously. You'll be helping me as much as I help you.

So.

Before we start.

I wanted to ask you. It's a bit. You know.

Is. Is anything going on between you and Rach?

Because she's fucking great you know. She's really helping me get through this. Well, you know.

And I wouldn't want to do anything about it if I was stepping on any toes. Or. Getting in the way of anything. So

Brief silence.

Cool. I didn't think so.

So.

Rach said you wanted to talk a bit about how I deal
with what's happened.

I don't know how much help I can be.

If you're anything like me you're in this place where
you're like 'why, why did this have to happen to me'
you know?

One thing that helps me get through the day is that every
morning I wake up and I dig deep inside myself and
I really interrogate how I'm feeling. You know? What's
going on in here. And once I've done that I know what
I can do for the rest of the day to keep myself right.

Sometimes it's as simple as going for a walk and
thinking yes. Mum might be gone.

But there is still a lot of good in the world. I'm still here.
I can still live. Breathe. Enjoy myself. Have a beer.

And

I'm alright. I'm okay.

So. I brought a pen and paper.
I wondered. If you felt comfortable.

Maybe you could start by writing down a few words
about how you've been feeling.

VIN *draws something.*

Okay.
So you've drawn a cock and balls.
That's great.
That's really.
That's funny.

Why don't we put the pen and paper away.

...

VIN *and* RACH.

RACH   You think you're a comedian?

VIN *hesitates. Nods.*

She punches him in the arm.

What's the matter with you?
He's just being nice.

VIN   **Yeah really nice.**

RACH   He sympathises

VIN   **Jamie's so nice.**

RACH   Why you being a dick?

        Don't you want to get better?

        Silence.

VIN   **Okay.**
        I'll do it.

RACH   Do what?

VIN   **A funeral for Dad.**

RACH   Oh.

        Really? You don't have to.

VIN   **Might be nice.**
        Just me and you?

RACH   If that's what you want.

        Just me and you.

                    ...

VIN *and* RACH. *The park with cans.*

RACH   Okay.

        Don't really know how to

        So. We're here today to celebrate the life of Phil.

Husband to Vicky.
Dad to Vin.
Dodgy electrician from what I hear.

Phil. Wish I'd met you.

But I know your son and if he's any reflection on you
then you must have been a top bloke. You're gone too
soon.

This is. This is something Vin text for me to read out.

'Dad

I miss you

Sorry for every time I was a dickhead
Every time I annoyed you
Or wasn't what you wanted me to be.

She pauses.

I don't know
How to say
What I need to
But

It feels like a bit of
me has sunk into
The ground
And I don't know how to get it out.

I don't remember
What things were like
When they weren't
Like this
And I wish they could go back.

I love you.

Your son.

Vin.'

Vin. Is that really how you feel?

That was really beautiful. I mean it.

Okay,

Cheers Phil.

They pour out their beer cans.

Shall we do a minute's silence?

Alright then.
Three
Two

They have a minute's silence.

They look at each other.

RACH *watches the last ten seconds.*

Right then.

Pub?

Is it alright if I invite Jamie? He's been having
a tough week.

...

The pub.

JAMIE   I've been having a tough week Vin.

Well you know how it is.

It comes in waves you know.
Some days I almost forget.
And then blam.

I remember.

Brief silence.

RACH   Shall I get the drinks in?

...

One drink in.

RACH   Cheers.
Vin would like to say sorry. About the cock-and-balls
thing. Wouldn't you Vin?

VIN *nods.*

JAMIE   Nothing to say sorry for.

RACH   Here's to your dad Vin.

JAMIE   To your dad.

They drink.

And my mum.

...

Two drinks in.

JAMIE   What d'you mean it's disappearing?

RACH   I mean it's fuckin' disappearing. Cheers.

Vin'll tell you.

The bus stop on Woodland Road. The top three floors of Welstead House. The fucking King Arms vanished last week. Well, half of it anyway –

The other half's still there but who wants to drink in half a pub you know?

JAMIE   How could that even be possible?

RACH   I don't know. But I'm gonna find out.

There's got to be a reason.

...

Four drinks in.

JAMIE   To the best fucking Mayor this town will ever have.

RACH   Fuckin' cheers to that

Jamie?

JAMIE   Yes mate.

RACH   Can I ask you something?

How do you not seem, you know, a mess?

JAMIE   Oh.

RACH   Sorry.
        Is that an annoying question? Bringing the mood
        down.

JAMIE   No. No.

RACH   It must be hard

JAMIE   It is.

RACH   No but it must be. You've been through a lot. I mean.
        Like. A lot.
        More than anyone I've met probably.
        And you seem so.

JAMIE   You know.

RACH   Together.
        No you do. You do. Doesn't he Vin?

        VIN *nods.*

        What was it like being there?

JAMIE   Oh.

RACH   You don't have to talk about it if you don't want to.

JAMIE   No. It's just.
        It's hard.

RACH   Of course.
        Sorry.

        Let's talk about something el–

JAMIE   The green light in the sky.

        That's what I remember.

        The sonic boom.

        The noise of car alarms.

        The sound of panic.

        Dad didn't even put his shoes on. His feet were all cut
        up from the glass. People were in tears, checking their
        phones. All the signal was wiped out. No one could
        tell what was happening.

We ran. This woman had cut her face. I yanked her up, hurt my thumb, calmed her down.

We could see it was bad. Everyone thought it was a nuclear bomb or something.

I still find it ridiculous. An asteroid.

It sounds made up.

RACH   That's what I kept saying! Didn't I Vin?

JAMIE   But it's not made up.

RACH   No.

JAMIE   It's not made up and people have died you know my mum has died and sometimes I feel like it doesn't actually matter that it was an asteroid that killed her you know it could have been anything it could have been a bus or cancer it's like the actual fact that she's dead that is the ridiculous thing. You know what I mean?

RACH   I think so.

JAMIE   But then other times I'm like 'an asteroid?'
Come on.
You've got to be kidding me.

When I saw my mum in the hospital... I didn't recognise her. Her hair was totally gone.
Her eyelids too. Her lips. The skin on her face was

But she looked at me and she recognised me. I could see the comfort it gave her. That will stay with me forever. I sat with her and gave her water and held her hand and she kept doing this thing with her mouth.

They told me it was a miracle she was alive this long.

Me and Dad took it in turns to be with her. She died in the night as I held her in my arms. I told her I loved her. Told her it was okay.

But in my head I just kept saying.

Please don't die.
Please don't die.

Please don't die.
I will give anything
Do anything
If you just don't die.

But she did.
There was nothing I could do to stop her.

RACH   Jesus. Jamie. I'm sorry.

She puts her hand on his.

JAMIE   You just sort of. Get on with it.

Vin understands, don't you mate?

Suddenly VIN *hits himself, open palmed, on the head. Slowly at first.*

RACH   Vin?

Then faster.

Vin what the fuck –

Vin.

Stop it

Stop it

He hits himself and then the table and then himself and then the table and then –

Fucking stop!

He stands up.

...

Outside the pub.

RACH   Hey.

What was that about eh?

Pretty intense story eh? Why don't you come back inside?

No.

Okay. Fuck off then.

He spills his guts in there and you're the one who
throws a strop? I know you're sad about your dad and
that but don't you think you've stretched things
a bit too far? I mean there gets to a point where it's
just fucking showing off you know it's all a bit look at
me look how sad I am I've stopped talking everybody
feel sorry for me.

Look at that guy in there. Look at what he's been
through.

I'm sorry to say it but it's fuckin'

true.

Long silence.

Vin. I'm sorry. I didn't mean that.
I want to have a conversation with you. Don't you
understand that?

Come back inside, eh?

Whatever.

It's cold.

I'm going back in.

...

VIN's *house.* JAMIE *is there.*

JAMIE   Rach gave me your address.

I wanted to say sorry.

I talk too much. I know that. Always have done.

I know everybody deals with these things differently.
And I'm sorry if that story. Upset you. Or.

She cares about you a lot, Rach.

You know. There's a part of me that actually enjoys
telling that story. Getting to the sad parts. Watching
people's reactions. What's that about?

Anyway I just wanted to make sure that I hadn't

VICKY *enters*.

VICKY   Vin?
Oh hiya.

JAMIE   Hello.

VICKY   I didn't mean to interrupt.

JAMIE   Jamie. Nice to meet you.

VICKY   I'm Vin's mum.
Vicky.

JAMIE   That is so cool.

VICKY   How do you two know each other?

JAMIE   We're mates.

I'm staying with Rachel.

VICKY   Rachel?
Oh is that her name?
Vin?

VIN *nods*.

Well.
I've heard a lot about Rachel. Apart from her name. So
thanks for that.

JAMIE   You haven't met?

VICKY   He's been keeping us apart.
Probably worried what I'll say.

JAMIE   She's an old family friend.
Been staying with her family since
I'm from London and my house was destroyed in

VICKY   Oh you're kidding. You were there?

JAMIE   That's right.

VICKY   Oh that's awful.
         And your family?

JAMIE   My mum. She passed.

VICKY   Oh no.

JAMIE   It's been a rough time.

VICKY   I've given to the appeal. Haven't I Vin?
         Donated clothes.

JAMIE   Thank you.
         We appreciate it.

VICKY   If I can ever do anything.

         I love London.
         I do.

         I was so sad to see that happen.

JAMIE   That's very kind.

VICKY   I hope you've got someone looking after you.

JAMIE   I do. Rachel's been so great.
         And Vin, of course.

         You know it's been a real support. Having someone
         who knows a bit about what I'm going through.

VICKY   Right.
         I'm not sure I

JAMIE   With his dad.

         Because they died around the same time.

VICKY   I

         His dad's not dead love.

         He's in Derby.

         Brief silence.

JAMIE   I'm. I'm sorry?

VICKY   He lives in Derby.

He's not dead. Least as far as I know. He was in Corfu last week or so the internet tells me.

Did he tell you he was dead?

Brief silence.

JAMIE   No.

Of course. Sorry.

I.
Misspoke.

VICKY   Okay. Because if he's been

JAMIE   No no it's me I misspoke. I got it wrong.
I was thinking of someone else.

VICKY   Right.

Okay.

Well.

I'll leave you to it.

Nice to meet you Jamie.

JAMIE   You too.

VICKY   Very sorry for your loss.

VICKY leaves.

Silence. JAMIE stares at VIN.

JAMIE   Mate.

...

VIN and RACH. JAMIE watches on.

RACH   Why did you lie?

I'm gonna ask you again Vin. Why? Actually now would be a fucking good time to say something.

What is wrong with you you fucking freak? Seriously?

SAY SOMETHING.

VIN *tries to text her.*

No. No don't text me. Don't fucking

You got something to say to me you can say it.
Out loud.

Oh, what's the point eh? Why bother. Why does
anyone bother trying to make things better why don't
we all just lie down in the muck and let it fucking
wash over us.

They can have this town. Delete it or steal it or
whatever they want. Let it disappear off the map for
all I care. Do you hear me whoever you are? Take it.
Take it all!

I'm done.

STAGE FOUR: DEPRESSION

Estimated death toll: 12,157.

VIN*'s house.* VIN *alone.*

Long silence.

Ages.

…

VICKY   Gus!
                 Gus!
                 Gus!
                 Gus!
                 Gus!
                 Dinner!
                 Gus!
                 Gus!
                 Gus!
                 Gus!
                 Gus!

…

You haven't seen the cat have you? He's still not back. I know it's silly but. I can't stop picturing him. Lost somewhere.

Or dead. Under the wheels of a car. Or or having crawled under a bush to die. Or with his legs broken. Or his little head squashed.

Silence.

I'm sorry love.

I don't know why I'm crying.

Silly really.

I honestly don't.

…

VIN *and* VICKY *sit in silence.*

Ages.

                      ...

VIN *in silence.*

Ages.

                      ...

VICKY   One of the neighbours found him.

Hit by a car I think.
He's not breathing, anyway. I know we didn't have
him long but

Long silence.

I'm.
I'm struggling a bit love.

I'm not gonna lie.

I don't know why but I'm having a bit of a tough

And it would be nice if
I need a bit of

No. Okay.

Do you know how hard it is?

To have nothing there. Nobody to talk to. To come
home and have the house filled with

It's getting to the point where I can't be around you
but I'm terrified to leave you alone. I don't know what
to do love.

Life's not that easy for any of us. You know that?
There's a big fucking blank space where my life was

supposed to have been and I don't understand how it got there. But you don't see me moping around like a fucking mute.

Turn on the news what about them. That friend of yours. Thousands of lives ruined by chance. But they're cleaning up. They got on with it. Bit of character, love, that's all.

Please. Talk to me.
Say something.
Anything.
One word

A noise even.

Just. Something.

Say something.

Say something.

Say something. Say something. Say something.
Say something. Say something. Say something.
Say something. Say something. Say something
say something say something say something say
something say something say something I can't do this
any more can't talk to myself any more I'm going
crazy I'm going fucking crazy.

I can't take

This

Silence.

I'm sorry.
I need you to

I need

...

RACH*'s driveway.*

RACH   Go home Vin. You can't just wait in my driveway.
Mum told you already.

What you did is actually a pretty fucked-up thing to do
to another person. Do you understand that? Especially
the only one who gives you the time of day.

I mean. We had a fucking funeral. It'd be funny if it
wasn't so

You must've known I would find out eventually. What
was your long-term plan?

Don't you understand you idiot?

I liked you.
A lot.
More than that even.

But I can't be your friend unless you're honest with me.

I can't help you if you don't tell me what's going on.
Nobody can.

She waits for a response.

No?

Then go home Vin. Please. And leave me alone.

Because it's fucking exhausting.

VIN *watches her leave.*

VIN *tries to speak.*

*He's furious. Wants to hit something. Or someone.
There's nothing to hit.*

The anger builds

Tries to scream

He can't

The anger builds

Tries to scream

He can't

The anger builds and builds and builds and he

Explodes

Furious with himself. With his throat his larynx his vocal cords. His tongue.

He tears at himself.

Hurts himself.

Tearing and hurting again and again smacking whatever is near to him his body the floor his body the floor then himself and then the floor and then himself and then the floor again and again punching his way to the core of the Earth the anger pouring out of every part of him until – until –

JAMIE   Vin?

         JAMIE is stood there in the driveway of the house he is staying in, holding a blue carrier bag.

         VIN looks at him.

         What you

         What you doing?

         I just bought some cans.

         Fancy one?

         I could

         I could really use a drink.

         ...

The two young men drink their cans.

JAMIE   Just spoke to my dad.
I'm going back to London.

My house has been declared safe. So that's. A relief.

Can't wait to get home. Cannot wait.

Cheers.

Brief silence.

Sorry I grassed you up.

Rachel still pissed?

VIN *looks at him.*

Yeah.

Although I'm not sure beating yourself up in her
driveway is the best way to

Fair enough.

I just. Don't understand why you would lie about
something that big.

Silence.

You know what. That's not true.

My mum. She didn't die in my arms. I told you she
did but

I mean I was there. In the burns unit. And I saw her
saw all her. Skin and that.

But I got to the door of her room and I could hear her
calling for me and I couldn't go in. And I turned to go
and my dad grabbed my hand but I wrenched it away
and I left the hospital.

I went and got chips and by the time I came back she
had died.

I dislocated my thumb. I wrenched my hand away so
hard that I dislocated my thumb. I don't know why
I lied about that.

Silence. JAMIE *wipes his eyes.*

State of the two of us eh? Jesus.

VIN *puts his hand on* JAMIE*'s shoulder.*

Cheers.

...

VIN*'s house.* RACH *and* VICKY. VICKY *is holding a cat basket.*

VICKY   So you're Rachel.

RACH   That's right.

VICKY   Rachel from the pub.

RACH   I guess so.

VICKY   Thanks for coming.

RACH   When I got your text –

VICKY   He's upstairs.

        Silence.

RACH   What's in the

VICKY   A cat.

RACH   Aw!

VICKY   He's dead.

RACH   Oh.

VICKY   I'm going to bury him in the garden.

        It's nice.
        Finally meeting you.

RACH   You too.

VICKY   Can I
        Does he. Does he talk to you?

RACH   Nah.

VICKY   Okay. That's what I thought.

RACH   Can I ask.
        And tell me if it's none of my business because it's
        usually not. But.
        What caused it?

VICKY   I'm sorry

RACH   The reason why he can't speak.
        I thought it was. Something else.

        But it's not that.
        So I was

        Was it to do with London?
        When he heard the news maybe?

VICKY   I don't think so.
        It's started about a week before.

RACH   Oh.

VICKY   This is the longest it's ever lasted.

RACH   It's happened before?

VICKY   He didn't tell you?

        When he was younger.
        I would notice him talking less and less.
        The words would drain away until
        And then one day they'd be back.
        It hasn't happened for years. I thought he'd grown out
        of it.

        This time's different. I don't know.

        He refuses to get help and I don't know what else
        I can

        I can't force him. You know?

        VIN enters. Stares at them.

RACH   Hiya Vin.

        I'm at your house.

        Brief silence.

VICKY   Well.

I better get on. This hole won't dig itself.

Nice to meet you Rach.

RACH   Sorry about your cat.

VICKY   It's alright.
        He wasn't really ours.
        Just a visitor really.

        VICKY *leaves.*

RACH   I wasn't gonna come but.
        Jamie convinced me.

        Still not texting me. Okay.

        You don't make it easy, do you mate?

        Silence.

        I've been thinking a lot about why you'd lie to me like
        that. Why anyone would lie about something like that
        when there are so many people going through terrible
        shit for real. And I was so angry with you. I'm still
        fucking angry with you.

        But I think part of it. At least. Is on me.

        I came round here to get you to tell me the truth. The
        real truth. I've always thought I could help you if
        I could find what was wrong.

        But it's not as simple as that. Is it?

        Look at me. Whatever's going on in there. However
        big or small or stupid you might think it is. You don't
        have to justify it. To me. Or to anyone.

        If you're feeling it.

        Then it's real. Okay?

Because there are people who will help you. You've only got to ask.

She waits for him to answer. Silence. Ages.

You know. Things are still going missing.

The other day I was in town and there was just this hole where a pavement slab should be. It wasn't dug up, there wasn't building works going on. All the other slabs were perfectly normal but where this one was was just this, deep, black hole. I stood there ages, kept waiting for someone to fall in, but they never did.

I'll see you Vin.

RACH *leaves.*

VIN *alone for a while.*

Silence.

VICKY *returns.*

VICKY   The strangest thing just happened. I'd finished digging the hole and I reached into the basket to take him out. And I lay him on the grass and thought. I'll give him a stroke just to say goodbye. Say some words.

And so I'm crying and I'm stroking him and I'm saying some words and then all of a sudden

He purred.

He purred and his tail started moving. And he got up. And he looked at me. And he walked away and climbed over the fence.

I don't know if he wasn't dead. Or he was dead and now he's not.

I wonder if that's ever happened before.

Seems

impossible.

Suddenly VIN *tries something. He hums, feeling the voice in the back of his throat.*

VIN   Mm

Mmmm

It is the first noise she's heard him make in months.

VICKY   Vin?

VIN   Mmmm

VICKY   What you

VIN   Mmmmmmmmmmmmmmmmmmmmmmmm
Mmmmmmmmmmmmmmmmmmmmmmmm
Mmmmmmmmmmmmmmmmmmmmmmmmmmmmmmmm
mmmmmmmmmmmmmmmm

VIN *suddenly breaks down crying. He cries into his mother's arms. He cries and he cries and he cries.*

VICKY   Hey. It's alright baby.
It's alright.
I got you.

Your mum's got you.

...

VICKY   I'm sorry I lost my temper the other day.
I know it's not your fault.

I just want you to be
Us to be

You know what?

Neither of us are doing that well, are we?

VIN   **Mum.**

VICKY   Oh.
You text me. You feel okay texting me?

She beams.

Well. That's. Okay.

VIN   **I need help.**

VICKY   What can I

VIN   **If I keep on like this I'm gonna**

        explode.

VICKY   Hey.
        It's alright.
        We'll sort something.

        Don't want you exploding eh? You'd wreck my carpet.

        Whatever help you need, we'll get it.
        I promise.

STAGE FIVE: ACCEPTANCE

Time since impact: 367 days 5 hours 4 minutes 11 seconds.

VIN *and* RACH.

RACH   Vin.

             Hiya. Thought that was you.

             Been ages. How you doing?

             Still not talking?

VIN   **Same number?**

RACH   Same number yeah.

VIN   **It's good to see you.**

RACH   You too.

             Brief silence.

VIN   **What's new?**

RACH   Quit the call centre.

             Looking at doing social work maybe. Think that might be alright.
Can't fix everything. But I can do a bit, you know?

             Still time to be Mayor one day.

VIN   **Get Jamie to write a campaign song.**

RACH   Oh god.

             He's back with his dad.
Keeps inviting me to stay with him but. I don't really fancy it.

VIN   **I'd like to see the crater.**

RACH   They've already started building on it.

             Can't believe it's been a year.

             It was the maddest thing and now it's just something that happened, you know what I mean?

VIN   **Rach.**

       I'm sorry.

RACH   Shut up.

VIN   **You were a good mate. And I lied to you.**

RACH   It was ages ago.
       How's it all going?

VIN   **Better.**

RACH   That's good.

       He puts his index finger up as if to say 'hang on'.

       He signs something in BSL.

       Shit. Is that real?
       What did it say?

VIN   **'Rachel for Mayor.'**

RACH   Amazing.

VIN   **I think.**
       Not very good yet.

RACH   You got some help?
       That's great Vin. That's really great.

       Brief silence.

       Did you see?
       Couldn't fucking believe it.
       Swimming pool's back. Slide and everything.
       Maybe they were only borrowing it.

VIN   **There's something I should say.**

       VIN *tries to speak. Takes a while. Struggles. Keeps*
       trying.

RACH   It's alright.

       I know.

       You don't have to.

       I should get off. I'm meeting

It's been good to see you mate. You look after
yourself, okay?

*He nods. She hugs him, and turns to walk away. And
then suddenly three words from deep inside* VIN *rise
to the top and erupt into the air between them.*

VIN   Thank.

You.

Rach.

She turns back.

*He seems surprised by his own voice. He tries it again.
Once more, more confidently this time, from the
bottom of his heart.*

The two friends smile at each other.

Thank you.

SKYSCRAPER LULLABY

Acknowledgements

Tom Martin and Andy Hughes and the National Theatre Studio for the baby steps.

Stephanie, Celia and Arian for shaping it and selling it so heartbreakingly.

Max Perryment who made something brilliant and freaky as hell.

And of course Emilia LaPenta, who is the reason that this baby grew into the monster.

Skyscaper Lullaby was released as an audio drama by Audible Originals on 8 December 2022. The cast was as follows:

DOCTOR	Stephanie Hsu
MOM	Celia Keenan-Bolger
DAD	Arian Moayed

Director	James Fritz
Producer and Dramaturg	Emilia LaPenta
Sound Designer, Audio Production and Music	Max Perryment
Casting	Chelsea Adams
Script Supervisors	Fiona Selmi and Jacob Morton
Additional Engineering and Mastering	David Holmes
Editor	Reel Audio Books
Executive Producers	Kate Navin and Emilia LaPenta
Head of Audible Studios	Zola Mashariki
Executive Vice President & Head of US Content	Rachel Ghiazza

Characters

DOCTOR
MOM
DAD

Note

Should probably be a noisy play.

It's a big idea, so go big with it.

The sounds of Taylor are open to interpretation. Some might be
lovely. Some might be horrifying. Some might be not what you
expect.

Prologue

DOCTOR   Wherever I go. Whoever I talk to.

I'm always asked the same question.

It doesn't matter what we're talking about, they'll always find a way to ask me.

What did it feel like?

Really?

What did it feel like, to be eaten alive?

The Father

Sounds of Taylor.

DAD   It's the not knowing.

That's what drives you crazy.

The not knowing what really happened.

The places your imagination goes to when it has to fill in the blanks.

I wouldn't wish it on anyone.

There's grief
There's loss and pain

And then

There's what we went through

Our son Taylor was born on a Wednesday on a sunny afternoon in Alameda Hospital.
Alameda is – was, before it was destroyed – a little island town across the bay from San Francisco. Nice houses, leafy, good people.

That feeling of holding him for the first time.

I felt so ready to be a father.

Sounds of Taylor.

Taylor was great, man. He was everything.

Silly, and strange, and smart, everyone said so.

He loved people. He was fascinated by them. So many other kids we knew back then, the only thing that would entertain them would be a a a screen, some cartoon, not that there's anything wrong with that, but. Taylor was never like that. That's all.

He was such a curious little boy, interested in the world. I always thought he might grow up to be an author or a journalist or

I don't know

A

Sounds of Taylor.

It's funny, the little things that stay with you.
He was always running round the park.
He was constantly saying hi to strangers.
His huge appetite. He would eat and eat.
The strength of his fingers when he held on to your hand.
The way he would play with the neighbour's cat.
The look in his eyes when he got sick and his mom would sing to him to make it better.

Sounds of Taylor.

I still see him, everywhere I go.

Just this week, I was standing in line at the market, and there he was, just ahead of me. I recognised the back of his head, his hair, the way he moved, and my heart jumped a beat and I moved towards him. And then he turned around, and of course, it was another little boy.

Every time it happens it hits me all over again that he's gone.

It's stupid. I know.

For one thing, Taylor would be fifteen years old by now. Fifteen! Sometimes I try and imagine what he might look like.
He might be taller than me, you know?

Which is

Sounds of Taylor.

It was a day just like any other.

He was four years old. His mother had a meeting in
the city. I'd taken the day off, which was rare, so
I decided that I would take Taylor on an adventure.

I thought I'd take him to one of my favourite hiking
spots, up in Montgomery Woods. It's beautiful up
there.
We parked and hiked
To this little clearing I knew, right among the
redwoods.

He was running around, and I left him playing at
being Spider-Man or something. Taylor loved it.

I sat down and watched him play in the trees. I lay
back on the ground
So I could get a better view.

I'd been working a lot of late nights. I hadn't been
getting much sleep and

I'm not making excuses, I'm just

I was watching him and

Sounds of Taylor.

And I remember laughing calling out

Sounds of Taylor.

And then
I don't know what happened.
I must have
Fallen asleep
Just for a moment.

Because my eyes closed, and when I opened them

Taylor?!

Taylor was gone.

I didn't panic; I knew he couldn't have gone far, so
I got up and just started walking around.
I couldn't see him anywhere.
All I could see were trees. Miles and miles of
fucking trees.

I started to get this little feeling of panic at the back
of my head, you know, but I told myself, ignore it,
you know, try and stay calm because he's going to
show up any minute right?

He's going to show up any –

And so I keep looking, but I don't know which
direction to walk in, so I call his name
Again and again and again
And I walk a little way in that direction
And a little way in this direction
But we're in the middle of nowhere.
And there's no sign of him.

There's no sign of him anywhere just trees and trees
and now the panic's building and time's ticking by
and after ten minutes my heart is racing, after
twenty I'm struggling to breathe I'm running in
different directions clutching at trees and branches
the stress the stress

And after half an hour I'm desperately trying to
shut up the thoughts in my head. Thoughts of a
future without him.

I looked for almost an hour before I called the
authorities. I don't know why I waited so long.
Hindsight.

And then, of course, I had to make the call to
Taylor's mom.

Sounds of Taylor.

It was crazy. There was a search across the forest.
By nightfall they still hadn't found him.

I remember thinking this can't really be happening,
I'm in a, I'm in a movie this is a scene from a
movie that I've seen before where the parents sit on
one side, and the police officer sits on the other and
says things like

'Anything you can tell us about your son.'

I remember
I told them that he needed a haircut.

I don't know why I thought that would help.

They keep telling you the first twenty-four hours
after a disappearance are crucial. But what they
really mean, what they don't tell you but Google
does, is that the first twenty-four hours are the only
time where they're looking for a child who's still
alive.

Sounds of Taylor.

It's hard to describe what those next few days and
weeks were like. It was purgatory.
You just sit around
Waiting for a phone to ring
To tell you what you already know.

Taylor's mom was –
Of course she was –
And I kept saying
I'm sorry
I'm so sorry.

And all she kept saying was things like
'It's not your fault' and 'It was an accident.'
But in her eyes –

Sounds of Taylor.

Weeks went by with no new leads.
We wanted to do one of those appeals you used to
see on TV, where we would go in front of the
cameras to ask for information. They told us they
don't do those any more.
They don't do them because every time they do, the
police get flooded with hundreds of false sightings
and there is too much to investigate.
People feel so sorry for the parents that they see the
missing child everywhere.

Most nights I would just go and lie on his bed.
The smell of his room.

The
The feel of his clothes.

I'd play out every possibility, every awful version
of his
Of how he might've

Sounds of Taylor.

Things with Taylor's mom became

Difficult.

The hardest thing was, I think, that it was
impossible to know what we should be doing.
We couldn't let ourselves grieve
Because that would mean that we had given up
hope.
We couldn't let ourselves hope
Because that would make the inevitable even harder
to deal with when it came.
So you just. Wait.

Sounds of Taylor.

She started to struggle.
Really struggle.

She sort of just stopped

Stopped sleeping
Stopped eating

Wouldn't
Really
Talk to me. Wouldn't talk about what happened.
Wouldn't even mention Taylor's name.
She would shut her eyes tight whenever she walked
past his room.

I don't know if it was the lack of sleep
Or what
But she increasingly started saying things
Things that wouldn't make sense.
Non sequiturs or strange references to events that
never happened.

Sounds of Taylor.

It was about three months after the disappearance
Taylor's mom came into our bedroom, sat me down
and took my hand. It was the first time she had
shown any affection to me since it happened, I think.
She took my hand and she said something like –

I just want to say something. I hate it when people
say she's crazy. Unless you've been through what
we've been through you have no idea. Don't call
her crazy. She's not crazy. The things it does to your
head. The pressure it puts you under.

Losing Taylor. It changed her.

She said while holding my hand,
'I've been thinking
And I want to tell the world the truth about Taylor.'
And so I said
'No, we – What truth? What are you talking about?'
And she got mad
And said
'Don't do that! You know exactly what I'm talking
about!'

And that's when she told me this
Horror story.

Sounds of Taylor.

Her grief is so overwhelming that it rewrote her
reality.
Rewrote it into an incredibly detailed, completely
fabricated version of the life of our son.
And the frightening thing was, she believed every
word.

Sounds of Taylor.

She's suffering from a form of psychosis brought on
by PTSD. It's when the brain detaches itself from
reality as an extreme way of coping with trauma.
Making it easier to process. That's what I read,
anyway.

She couldn't cope with what happened to Taylor, so
her mind rewrote her history, Taylor's history, to
make him seem –
Awful.

So unimaginably awful that it would make the idea
of losing him
Easier to deal with.
Which breaks my heart. You know?

Sounds of Taylor.

In the end, it became too hard.

These fantasies, they took over our lives.
I couldn't convince her it wasn't real, couldn't
convince her to get help.
I told her that I loved her and I hoped she would get
the help she needed. I prayed that she would be able
to remember our son the way that I remembered
our son.

I sat across from her on our bed. I told her I was
sorry, but that I couldn't be the one to get her
through this.

I wish I could remember Taylor more clearly.
I promised myself that I would keep my all my
memories fresh in my mind but

Time

Now I've only got snatches. A couple of videos on
my phone.

When there's no one else you can talk with about a
person then their memory starts

Slipping. It just starts slipping away.

Sounds of Taylor.

My life today is very different.
After the divorce I took a job in Portland.

I met someone, remarried.
We have two beautiful daughters. I have told them all
about their bigger brother, who they'll never meet.

A decade went by, somehow.

And then on the morning of 29th October I woke up

To a text message
saying Taylor was alive.

The Mother

MOM   I'm not crazy.

I'm not.

I know that's what everyone thinks. There she goes that woman who lost her mind when her son disappeared.
But that's not what happened.

I've got proof of that now.

Sounds of Taylor.

My story is

Fucking unbelievable. I know that.

But
Given everything that's happened these last few years. Given everything the world has been through.

Maybe it's time our definition of 'unbelievable' was rewritten. You know?

Sounds of Taylor.

When my son Taylor was born, on a Tuesday in Alameda

He was born with three teeth.

The doctor told us that he had never seen anything like it. Three teeth on a newborn which when you're breastfeeding –
But I didn't mind. Really. I found it cute.
He was our little smile guy.
I always suspected Taylor's dad never really wanted kids.
I think he went along with it because that's what you were supposed to do, right? You reached a

certain age and a certain wage and it makes sense to
become a parent so you do it, and you hope it's the
right choice and you hope that you're good at it.
But me, I knew.
I always knew I wanted to be a parent. That it
would make me happy. And that I'd be good at it.
It's easy to forget, after everything that's happened,
but we had two years with Taylor before the change
began, where we were just a normal family.
Two years of happiness.
I think back on that time every day.

Sounds of Taylor.

It was Taylor's nanny, Rosa who first noticed
something was wrong.

She was amazing. She started looking after Taylor
when he was about a year old. We were both back
at work full time and we wanted someone who
could help around the house.

She was what you would call *a* character. She came
from Guatemala and had all these old-wives tales
for getting a baby to sleep through the night.

She told me that the reason that we sing lullabies
isn't to calm the baby down, it's to calm the parent.

(*Sings.*) 'And if that mocking-bird won't sing,
Mama's gonna buy you a diamond ring.'

Singing regulates the breathing and makes the
parent seem relaxed when they're holding the baby,
and then the baby knows that there's no danger, and
so it has an easier time falling asleep. I thought that
was amazing.

Rosa was always really classy. She would come to
work dressed like a fifties movie star, wearing these
emerald-blue dress shoes every day of the week.

Some nights, after Taylor had been put to bed, she
would stay late and we would sit down on the
couch, share a bottle of wine and she would tell me
stories of her life.

I really liked her. So when she came to us out of the blue, sat us down and said that she thought Taylor had a serious problem,

Well, I listened.
I asked her what sort of problem

And then she said 'A problem with meat'

Meat?

You mean, like. Meat meat?

She said, every time he saw a piece of meat, every time she roasted a chicken or took a steak out of the fridge, he would go crazy, like a wild animal.
She said in all her years as a nanny, she had never seen a child behave like this.

'Please' she said. 'You must have someone look at him.'

I told her that he just saw his paediatrician and everything was fine.

Rosa said she didn't mean a doctor should look at him.

She said she meant a priest.

Sounds of Taylor.

You know, it's easy to say that we should have done something about it, but we had never seen any of the things she was talking about. So.
I didn't know if she was imagining it or trying to be funny or making it up for attention or –

To me Taylor seemed like a normal little boy and Whatever Rosa had seen, I couldn't see it. So we just carried on.

Sounds of Taylor.

A few months later I came home to find Rosa at the kitchen table, talking to Taylor's father. She looked pale. She kept saying that she wanted to quit.

I was shocked.
I asked her what was wrong.
And she went very quiet.

And then she told the story.
She said Taylor had been playing in the backyard.
When she heard a noise
And she looked over
And saw that he had something
In his grasp.
And it was wriggling
And shrieking
And when she looked closer

When she looked closer
She saw
It was the neighbour's cat.
Anchovy.

Taylor didn't have the cat in his arms.
He had it in his mouth.
He had the throat of this cat
In his mouth
And he was shaking it
Like a rabid dog.

How is anyone supposed to react to a story like that?

I said
Rosa
I don't think you saw what you think you saw.
Because I just saw Anchovy out front and he's fine!
There wasn't a scratch on him.

Which wasn't true but, I wanted to make her feel better. I was worried she was having some sort of breakdown or

A few days later there was a knock on our door.
It was the neighbour come to tell us that her cat was missing, and if we saw it, could we let her know.

Sounds of Taylor.

We refused to accept Rosa's resignation. There was
no point losing someone so wonderful over what
seemed such a silly story.
The only way we could get her to stay was offering
her a fifty per cent raise. She said no at first, of
course, but eventually came round.
She needed the money.

It's easy to look back, knowing what we know now,
with the world the way it is.
But at the time
It didn't seem like a big deal.

Sounds of Taylor.

It was a month or so later when everything changed.
It was our wedding anniversary, so we left Taylor
with Rosa and headed into the city for dinner and
drinks. It was a tradition of ours, we would go back
to this Japanese restaurant, the same restaurant
where Taylor's father proposed to me.

I remember, I remember it was a beautiful San
Francisco evening. The sky. We had just finished
our dessert, when Rosa called me.

She was panicking.

She told us that Taylor had suddenly developed
some sort of fever.
She said his temperature was high, and he looked
like something was off, and we should come home
as fast as we could.

Sounds of Taylor.

When we got back to the house. Everything was
quiet.
It was.

Eerie.

Everything was quiet.

No Rosa.
No Taylor.

Taylor's dad noticed it first. There was a leak in the
ceiling, coming from upstairs. Like someone had
left the water running
We called out their names. *Rosa! Taylor!*
But there was no reply.

Together, we looked for them upstairs, still calling
out their names.

The landing was flooded. Water was pouring out
from under the door of the bathroom.

It was only
When I turned on the lights
I saw that it wasn't just water.
It was mixed with

With blood.

And then suddenly we heard this noise, coming
from inside the bathroom. It was like nothing I'd
ever heard.

Taylor's dad, knocked and slowly pushed open the
door.
The first thing that we saw
In a pool of blood and water
Were two emerald-blue dress shoes.

Rosa.

She was badly hurt. Torn up.
Her hair was all matted. The skin on her face was
all cut up and one of her eyes had sort of

She was struggling to breathe.

When I looked down I saw
She was
Missing her left hand
Severed at the wrist.
While her right hand was pressed against her
stomach where I could see her
Insides.

And then
Then my eyes fell on the corner of the room.
Where I saw

my son,

cross-legged.

Gnawing
On Rosa's severed hand

Like it was a candy bar.

Sounds of Taylor.

Sounds of Taylor.

Sounds of Taylor.

Of course, I started screaming.

I screamed and screamed and screamed. I screamed
like people only scream in the movies. I screamed
and I clawed at my face and I clawed at the walls
and I kicked at the air and I hammered on the
ground and I screamed and I screamed and
I screamed until I couldn't breathe any more

And by the time I was done, Rosa was dead.

Sounds of Taylor.

The next thing I remember, Taylor's dad was
washing the blood from him in the shower.

He kept saying
I need to get him clean
He was scrubbing the blood off Taylor so hard
Taylor was sobbing.

I remember I kept shouting
'You're hurting him!'

Sounds of Taylor.

We were sitting downstairs in the TV room. Still in
our anniversary clothes which were now soaked in
blood.

Rosa's body was still upstairs.
Taylor, washed and in clean pyjamas, was fast
asleep on the couch, like nothing had happened.
His dad just kept saying, over and over
Call the police.
We have to call the police, right?
And I said, yeah, let's call the police.

But neither of us picked up a phone.

Sounds of Taylor.

We'd bought the video monitor when he was first
born. It was always pointed at his bed to check that
everything was okay.

The footage was stored on an app on my phone.

We sat down together and watched back the last few
hours.

You could see Rosa
Coming into the room
Holding Taylor in her arms.
She puts him down
She goes out to start running a bath
She comes back
Taylor starts tossing and turning.
She makes the phone call, telling us to come home.
She brushes his hair with her fingers
And then
Suddenly

Sounds of Taylor.

We couldn't watch any more.
I can't remember which one of us said it first.
We couldn't
Couldn't show that footage to anyone.
They'd take him away from us.

We pressed erase.
And I burst into tears.

Sounds of Taylor.

We decided
that the next morning
We would take Taylor to the hospital
And let them run every test they could to find out
what was wrong with him.
But right now
We needed to get Rosa
Out of our house. Without anyone seeing. For
Taylor's sake. This was all for Taylor's sake.

Sounds of Taylor.

Carefully, gently, we carried Rosa downstairs and we
put her in the trunk of the car. He drove her out and
buried her in the woods about an hour east of
Alameda. We would go there sometimes on Sundays.

I stayed home with Taylor. I was terrified to be left
alone with him. He kept crying. At first I yelled at
him and I said

'I'm not coming anywhere near you! Look what
you did!'

But he kept crying and crying and crying. And of
course, I realised he didn't understand. He didn't
know what he'd done.

(*Sings.*) 'Hush little baby don't say a word...'

Sounds of Taylor.

The sun was up by the time Taylor's dad got home.
We went to the paediatrician. When the doctor
asked what we thought was wrong we tried to be as
vague as possible.

They found nothing wrong whatsoever. A healthy
little boy.

It was a relief in one sense, but –
And then we just. Took him home.

Sounds of Taylor.

The weeks went by.

We lived in fear.

Fear of Taylor doing it again.

Fear of the police coming knocking, for someone to come looking for Rosa 'Have you seen this woman? Where were you the night of.'

But the knock never came.

Taylor showed no sign of abnormality. Nothing at all.

I constantly googled looking for similar stories. Babies and toddlers who had grown especially strong, or done violent things. But there wasn't anything like this.

As time went by, as crazy as it sounds, we started to rationalise it.

It had been an accident, we had dealt with it. You can't blame a child that young for whatever this was so

We were sad for Rosa, so sad for Rosa but
It felt like there was nothing else we could do.

I really believe that with enough time we might have just gone back to normal, carried on with our old lives.

But then, of course. Taylor got sick again.

Sounds of Taylor.

It was about three months later.

I was making Sunday dinner and Taylor was sitting at the table with his crayons.

I looked over and I realised
Very quickly
That
Something was wrong. Something was horribly wrong.

His little hands had started clutching at the air, he was struggling for breath like he was choking on

something. His face had gone purple-grey and his
skin had gone
Shiny
And sort
Of
See-through.

We wrapped him up in a blanket and I called an
Uber to the emergency room.

Sounds of Taylor.

By the time it arrived Taylor was getting worse and
worse.

The Uber driver, I wish I could remember his name.
He kept saying, 'Don't worry little man, I'll get you
there, I'll get you there.'

Taylor's dad kept googling his symptoms.
The whole way I just kept stroking Taylor's hair
and saying don't worry, don't worry. I'm here.

We were about ten minutes from the hospital when
Taylor suddenly went limp in my arms. Like a little
rag doll. It was so frightening I thought he was dead
I was begging with him, pleading with him to
regain consciousness.
And then
Just like that
He did.
He
Flailed his arms, thrashing around, trying to get
away from me
And then he started making this
Noise.
The Uber guy turned around to see the commotion,
and of course he took his eyes off the driving and –

We ran right off the road.

We were fine, we were all okay, but the driver had a
gash on his forehead and before I could say anything
There was a blur
As Taylor hurled himself

From my arms
Towards the front seat.

It was chaos

The driver screamed,
We both tried
We really tried to wrench him off, but his arms, his
mouth was like a vice, he was so strong, too strong
how could he be that strong

Before we could stop him
Taylor put his tiny hands across
Across the driver's throat

And ripped it apart.

There was nothing we could do. We got out of the car.
We got out of the car and we closed the door behind
us, we closed our eyes tight and we put our hands
over our ears and we waited until it was all over.

Sounds of Taylor.

Sounds of Taylor.

Sounds of Taylor.

Sounds of Taylor.

By the time we opened the car door, the driver was
There were pieces of him all over the

But Taylor.

Taylor was fine.
He was smiling, and laughing. The fever, or
whatever it was, was gone.
A miracle cure.

Sounds of Taylor.

Taylor's dad got rid of the body and the car.
Of course we wanted to get some help, of course we
wanted to find some way of making Taylor better.

But what if they took him away from us?

What if he hurt someone again?

All we could do was watch him closely and pray
that it didn't happen again. And of course, he went
back to his usual self. Smiling, and playing, he was
so curious, 'What's this, Mama? What's this?'
For a little while, you know, we thought that maybe,
just maybe, that was it. He'd stopped and we were
in the clear.

And then, of course, the fever came back.

Sounds of Taylor.

His eyes. His face.
His breathing, it was all the same as before.
We decided to wait it out. We tucked him up in bed,
and tried everything to make him better. Tried
feeding him meat, cooked steaks, chicken, raw liver.
But as the night went on

It was obvious.

If we didn't do something our little boy was
Going to die.

Sounds of Taylor.

I don't regret what we did next.
I hate myself for it. But I don't regret it.
It was the middle of the night. We were sitting there
in the dark watching Taylor's chest rising and
falling, slower and slower. And I remember thinking

I
I can't do this.
I can't sit here and watch my my son die what kind
of mother would that make me?

What kind

of mother.

And so
Quietly
I kissed him on the forehead

And I, I got up and I went downstairs and I got into
our car and I drove into Oakland, and I drove

around until I saw a guy an old guy, he was
homeless at least it looked like he was, I said hello
and I told him that I had a hot meal and a warm bed,
and he got into the car and I drove him back to the
house and while I was driving I started to cry and
the homeless man said something like

'Don't cry, it'll be alright, God is watching'

And I don't know why he said that.

We got back to the house and I invited him inside
and I said would you like anything to drink and he
said warm cocoa if you have it, so I made him some
cocoa and gave him a plate of food, and then I said
if you go out to the garage there is a bed and some
clean clothes all set up for you, and then I went
upstairs and I picked up Taylor and he was still so
sick, he was so so sick and I then I took him down
to the garage and I introduced him to the old man
and I turned my back as he ate him alive.
And of course, after that, Taylor was fine.

Sounds of Taylor.

Sometimes I wonder whether everything,
everything that has happened since, is me being
punished for what I did to him.

Sounds of Taylor.

After that day the fevers kept coming back.
Every three months. Like clockwork.
Exactly the same. Purple face, hard to breathe,
yellow eyes. And every time we knew that the only
thing, the only thing we could do for him was –
Take care of it.
To the outside world that we were just a normal
family. And most of the time, we were.
We went to work. We came home. We watched TV.
We made dinner. We lived our lives just like anybody
else except every few months Taylor would get sick,
one of us would go out and find someone who
nobody would miss, bring them home and take them
down to the garage. Where Taylor would be waiting.

It's not like we wanted to do this. It's not like this
was the life we had dreamt of. We were taking care
of our son.
And we were, we were protecting people.
The way we saw it, it was better to keep Taylor
contained, to keep the fevers under control and limit
the people he was exposed to, than to let him out
into the world, unchecked. Who knows what could
have happened?
It was awful for the people that we chose. But
It was the right course of action.

Sounds of Taylor.

Somehow we lived like that for two years. In that
time Taylor ate fourteen people. I still know their
names by heart.
Every time he got sick we told ourselves that this
would be the last time. But then every time we
thought about losing him and
The funny thing is
For the most part. He was beautiful. He was our
beautiful little guy and I was so happy being his
mother. I thought his father felt the same.

Sounds of Taylor.

It was a Tuesday. Just a Tuesday.
It had been about a week since Taylor's last feed.
His dad had the day off so he offered to take him
out for an adventure. He never did that any more, so
I remember being pretty thrilled.
I waved them off and I went to work.

About four p.m. he called me.
I asked if they were having a good time but I could
hear, in his voice –
He was crying.
And then he told me.

He told me that something had happened.
He told me that he was sorry, but he couldn't take it
any more,

he couldn't take being around Taylor any more

and so he had taken our little boy to the middle of the woods,

all alone

And left him there.

**A Doctor at Zuckerberg General Hospital, During the
Devastating Attack on San Francisco by the Unidentified
Large-Scale Aggressor**

1. Hospital

A busy hospital.
A low rumbling.
The sound of the something terrifying from a few miles away.
A distinctive roar. The roar the whole world knows by now.

DOCTOR   That sound again.

         It's getting closer.

         Ignore it.

         Focus on the patient. Hold still for me. That's great –

         Don't think about what's going on outside. Don't
         think about –

         The rumbling continues. Sounds of terror, far away.

2. Memory

We move into a memory. A better time.

         It is the morning of 29th October.

         And I'm sitting on the toilet
         and I'm losing my mind.

         It is the morning of 29th October and I'm sitting on
         the toilet losing my mind because two things have
         just happened.

         The first is that the pregnancy test
         That I'm holding in my hand
         Has just shown up
         As positive.

This is not a faint inconclusive maybe/maybe not
sort-of-positive it is a big fat HD four-K you-are-
very-fucking-pregnant plus sign.
Which is
You know
Ordinarily would be
Huge but
Right now feels kinda insignificant because

The second thing that has just happened
The second thing

Is that my phone has just told me that a three-
hundred-foot monster has just started attacking
Japan.

Yeah.

I watch the clip for the fifth time in a row.

It shows something that sorta looks like an
enormous dinosaur crossed with a teddy bear
As it rises out of the ocean
Stands to its full height
And roars.

What the fuck. Is that.

Steve's voice rings out from the other room.

'Holy fucking shit.
It's as big as a skyscraper!
Babe you gotta come see this!'

I pull up my pants.
Pick up the test
And open the bathroom door to a very different
world.

3. Hospital

A rumbling in the distance.
The hospital. She surveys the waiting area. There are patients
everywhere: on the benches, the floor, in doorways.

It's five miles away.
Somewhere near Pacific Heights.
That's what Dr Peters said.

How long does that mean we have?

The ER is falling apart.
We need to get everyone out of here. We can't treat
them all. We need to get everyone out of h–

4. Memory

A memory.

'I can't believe it. I really can't believe it.'

Steve really can't believe it.

It is the afternoon of 29th October

The positive pregnancy test has made itself at home
on the coffee table in front of us, the news from
Japan playing out on the TV in the background.

They have started calling the monster
The Unidentified Large-Scale Aggressor.
ULSA for short, which I don't think is very catchy
but

I hear a news guy say that they still don't know
what it is or where it came from. 'How can they not
know what it is? They have to know!'

But Steve isn't listening. He's talking about
timelines and scans and how this is actually pretty
good timing for us to get pregnant because when
the baby is due he won't be too busy at work and –

He's so excited. It's sweet. And then he asks me if
I feel the same.

And we've been talking about this of course we've
been trying for months and so I look into his eyes
those big goofy eyes and I say yeah
Yeah
Of course I'm so excited

I'm so

But then I look up at the TV just as it starts to
show –

5. Hospital

This delivery driver is going to die.
There's nothing I can do
The delivery driver is going to die
still in his uniform
That logo that logo that I see on the streets every
day that has been at our door a hundred times is
Caked in blood torn to shreds
If we had his blood type
But we ran out an hour ago.
So he's going to die.
I'm sorry. I'm so sorry.
Next patient.

6. Memory

It's November 1st.

Three days since the appearance of the ULSA and
I'm working the night shift in the ER.

Doctors, nurses, patients, families: all anyone is
talking about is Tokyo Tokyo Tokyo
The ULSA won't stop eating people. Scooping
them up into its gigantic mouth dozens at a time.
An estimated hundred thousand are dead. Millions
more are homeless.
I have become a ULSA expert in the past two days.
I've read every article. Watched every clip.
Read every crazy theory about what it might be and
where it might have come from.
Alien, undiscovered sea creature,
Physical embodiment of Satan, US government
experiment, Chinese weapon of mass destruction.

The largest creature on earth and before this week
no one had ever seen it which is

crazy

Right before the end of my shift a woman is admitted
to the ER with two slit wrists. She keeps telling
everyone that the ULSA is the beast from the Book
of Revelations that heralds Armageddon. She was
trying to get to the front of the line for the rapture.

As soon as I'm done, I look up the relevant passage.

'Then I stood on the sand of the sea. And I saw a
beast rising up out of the sea, having seven heads
and ten horns, and on his horns ten crowns. Now
the beast which I saw was like a leopard, his feet
were like the feet of a bear, and his mouth like the
mouth of a lion.'

And stupidly I'm relieved because it doesn't look
anything like –

7. Hospital

The hospital nurse's station.

(*On the phone.*) Hi… hi thank god… I'm a doctor
from Zuckerberg General and they said I should
speak to… no listen to me, Sergeant, we need a
restock of anything you can spare… gauze, plasma,
antibiotics… I understand… I understand but we
have a ward overflowing with patients and we need
to find a way to…

8. Memory

It is three a.m. on November 5th.

I can't sleep.
I have to be at the hospital in four hours but my
brain is busy and I'm doom-scrolling scrolling
scrolling scrolling the news in Japan

A family's home on fire
Ten things to think about in your first trimester.
The ULSA swatting a helicopter out of the –
Dos and don'ts for first-time parents.
A claw crushing a tank in one swift –
What size is a fetus at six weeks
A row of enormous sharp teeth filmed through the
window of the sixty-second floor –
Traffic jams
Buildings collapsing
Schoolchildren running
Best school districts in the Bay Area
A mother crying
A father crying
A skyscraper falling
A mother crying
Two parents crying
Five hundred thousand dead, and rising rising rising
ri–

'Hey'

Steve's voice cuts through my busy brain.

'You should stop watching that stuff, it's not good
for you'

And he puts his arms around me and I put my
phone away and suddenly it doesn't feel so –

9. Hospital

Exhausted
Can't
Think

Sixteen hours straight

Maria is saying a prayer under her breath.

That new nurse
What's her name?
Is crying in the corner

I need to get back out there

They just brought a girl in
Crushed by a stampede of people
Fleeing for their lives.

I need to get back out there –

10. Memory

It is the evening of November 13th.
Steve and I are eating pizza and watching the news
coverage of the nuclear strike.

The CNN guy explains that the majority of the
population of the Shinjuku Tokyo area has been
evacuated in anticipation of the strike.

The majority
Which means there's still a minority that they're
going to vaporise.

'Can you imagine'
I say
'We might actually be bringing a kid into this mess'
Steve ignores the question and takes another slice.

The nuclear missile is designed
To burrow its way through
The skin of the ULSA
And explode
From the inside.
Which is fucking gross
But of course we're looking forward to seeing what
it looks like on camera.
But when the nuke hits its target
All there is is white light and the sound of wind

The ULSA screams out in pain and somebody on
the footage says direct hit! Direct!

Steve claps his hands together, pumps his fists and
shouts 'Come on!'
But suddenly I feel kinda sad
For the poor dumb thing. He doesn't know what's
going on! He doesn't know why he's been
exploded! He was probably just hungry

and

lost.

There is some triumphant babbling from the news guys when suddenly the smoke clears and the whole world sees that

the ULSA

is still there.

Unharmed. Not a scratch on it.

It opens its arms to the world
Like it's saying

'That all you got?'

This is the moment that everyone realises.

They can't stop it.

This thing is just gonna keep going and going and going and

11. Hospital

(*Doing CPR.*) No no no

I need some help over here she's in asystole!

One two three four
One two three four
One two three four
One two three four
One two three four

One two three –

Oh God no, Come on.

We need epinephrin. Has anyone seen any fucking epinephrine?
w

12. Memory

November 15th.

Steve and I are eating tacos in the Mission District because it's date night.

Steve asks me if I think that this taco place is better than the taco place we usually go to because the taco place we usually go has the tacos with the

'Aren't you worried'

I ask him

'about how we'll cope when the baby comes, you know, with both our jobs and our tiny apartment and lack of any savings and and and'

And he says

'Nah.'

Just like that.

'Nah. We'll cope. People always cope, don't they? There's no good time to have a baby.'

'No,' I say
'But there's definitely a bad time.'

And suddenly, I'm on a roll.

'I mean, they already fired one nuke at this thing. What if the ULSA leaves Japan and moves on to North Korea, what then? Or what if it destabilises Pakistan and then a terror group gets its hands on their nukes I read that could happen. Or what if it destroys a biolab and unleashes a plague, or what if none of that happens but it just keeps eating and eating and eating until there's nothing left, I mean do we really, do we really want to bring a child into that world?'

'That's all very hypothetical'

Er, yes Steve

Of course it's fucking hypothetical, everything
about the future is hypothetical that what makes it
the fucking future.

And that's when he says

'Let me ask you something. You're a doctor. Why
bother saving all those people's lives every day, if all
they have to look forward to is such a shitty future?'

He's so pleased with his argument I could –

'Look,' he says, 'The way I see it, people have had
babies in far worse times than this. The question we
should be asking is not whether our child might
want to be born into an unstable world full of three-
hundred-foot-tall monsters, because it's kinda
presumptuous for us to answer that on their behalf.
The only question that matters is whether we want
to have a child. Me and you.'

Yeah, I say. Of course we do. Of course.

13. Hospital

I can't find her

The little girl's mother

I can't find her anywhere
I need to tell her what happened.
I need to tell her I tried my best
I need to tell her that I couldn't
I couldn't –

I couldn't

14. Memory

On the morning of November 28th
Steve and I watch with the rest of the world as the
ULSA turns and heads back to the ocean, where it
swims to the deep.
The attack on Tokyo, over at last.

We should go out and celebrate, says Steve.
We should go to –

But suddenly I

Suddenly I feel

Steve…
Something's
Something's not right.

It's always awkward when a doctor has to be a
patient in their own hospital.

Elena from Obstetrics who's usually so fucking
rude is now being sickeningly nice to me, which is
worse if anything. She tells us it's very common
with a first-time pregnancy and we didn't do
anything wrong and the good news is we got
pregnant in the first place and and and

And right then I get a notification on my phone.
They've lost track of the ULSA.
It has vanished completely from all radar. The
world's largest creature,
Lost down the back of the couch. How does that
even –

Steve takes my hand and I realise he's crying.

But I'm not.

It's later that night, after one too many beers, that
I say it:

'Isn't there any part of you
Any small part of you

That's a little bit

Relieved?'

15. Hospital

She moves from patient to patient.

> – thirteen-year-old male with severe damage to the
> Can I get a crash cart over
> Charge it to three-sixty
> I'm sorry there wasn't anything we could –
> BP one-three-four over seventy-eight
> I'm trying I
> Shot in the abdomen entry and exit wounds
> One milligram morphine
> I don't know I I
> I need a surgeon please I need a
> Has anyone got any morph–

16. Memory

> I am so tired
>
> It is December 12th, and Steve and I have been stuck in the same conversation for days.
>
> 'I just want to know how you feel?'
>
> Out of habit I check my phone and go straight to CNN.
>
> No sightings.
>
> 'Because if we can't be honest with each other – '
>
> no sightings anywhere.
>
> It's been gone for two weeks now.
> Check Reddit
> Nothing
> Twitter
> Nope.
> I feel ashamed how much I miss it. I miss reading about it. Miss watching it.
>
> 'Are you even listening to me?'
>
> Yeah. Of course I am.

'When you say you don't want children, do you
mean, you don't want them now, or you don't want
them ever or?'

I...

How can something like that just disappear?

17. Hospital

There is a roar. Much closer now. Everyone stops.

It's two miles away.
Two miles and coming closer.

Someone's gonna need to get these bandages
changed –
Let me just –

Don't worry about it.

It roars.

Ignore

Keep going.

Deep breath
Who's next
You have to
keep –

It roars again.

Going

18. Memory

It is January 2nd.

Steve is still sleeping on the couch, because he
hasn't been able to find his own apartment yet.

It's six a.m. and I am about to leave for the hospital
but before I do

Hawaii.
The Pacific.

I want to wake him up and tell him

They found it.
They found it.

And they think that it's headed towards the Bay
Area. Towards us.

I want to tell him that I'm frightened
I want to tell him that I love him
And that I don't know how we got to this point and
I wish we could just go back to being –

But I don't.

I don't wake him up and I go to work and I let him
find out the news for himself.

19. Hospital

Wait

The sound of the ULSA's breathing, very loud.

Quiet.
Just quiet, for a second.

The breathing.

Did you hear that?
It's outside.
Doesn't that sound like it's right outside?

20. Memory

It is February 13th.

San Francisco is emptying. They are trying to move
twenty million people inland before the ULSA
reaches the Bay Area.

Steve is booked on an evacuation shuttle. It's going
to take him to a refugee camp near Modesto.

I walk him to the pick-up point.
Neither of us say anything until –

Come with me. Come with me, he says.

I can't. They need me at the hospital.

I try and shut down the thought that this might be
the last time I ever see him but I

How did we get here? How did we let it get this far?

I watch him get on the bus and the bus drive away
and

The very next day
I am in my scrubs
Watching on the break-room TV
As the monster
Rises up from the water
And destroys the Bay Bridge.

By two p.m. the hospital is already at capacity.
We are running out of supplies.
Most patients have not been injured by the ULSA.
They've been injured in the rush to escape the city.
Crowd crushes.
Stray bullets.
Car accidents.

I have seen more people die in one day
Than I have in my whole career.

We are overrun

We are overrun and the sound of the monster keeps
getting closer

21. Hospital

The sound of the monster is still right outside.

> Don't make it sound like a goodbye don't make it
> sound like a goodbye don't make
> it sound like a –

(*She leaves a voicenote.*) Hey, Steve… I… I wanted
to check in and let you know… I'm okay… things
are crazy in the hospital obviously but we're…
uh… But I… I just wanted to say… I just wanted to
say…

Shit

A rumble. The floor vibrates. Boom.

Holy shit the floor is shaking it's

*The floor vibrates. Boom. Boom.
The ULSA ROARS!*

I need to get out of here.
We need to go now

We need to get this hospital evacuated
Right now!

*Sound of the monster. A crowd starts to move.
People starting to panic.*

(*Shouts.*) Listen up, people, come on, we need to
get moving!

Sound of the monster. More panicking.

Need to get out need to get out of –

Sound of the monster.

Wait

Sound of the monster. Breathing.

Stop.

Stop.

There
That shadow
At the window.

It's above the building.

Sound of the monster.

(*Whispers.*) It's right above us.

Sound of the monster.

(*Whispers.*) Please. Please. Go away. Please.

Sound of the monster.
The sound grows faint.

Oh god. Oh thank you god.
It's gone. Okay.
It moved on.

We're okay. That was –

THE MONSTER IS HERE!
She runs through the collapsing hospital. It starts to destroy the building. Rips the ceiling off. It's right above us.

Oh jesusjesuschristjesusfuckingchrist move move
oh my god

The walls start to collapse.

The building's coming down! Run, you gotta, gotta
Ah shit get up go go run

The ceiling collapses.

Oh shit oh shit oh shit Don't look
Keep running
Run! Run fucking run! Oh jesus oh jesus

SOUND OF THE MONSTER.
SOUND OF THE MONSTER.
SOUND OF SCREAMING EARS RINGING
CHAOS EVERYWHERE.

That noise
So loud
Run
Keep running

SOUND OF THE MONSTER.
THE SOUND OF THE MONSTER. IT'S
DEAFENING.
IT BREATHES RIGHT ABOVE HER.

Oh

It's right above me.
It's right above me.
It's right above me.
It's.
No no plea–

*WHOOSH. THE MONSTER ENVELOPS
EVERYTHING.*

22. The Mouth

Sounds of chaos.
Sounds of a body.
Sound of complete silence.
And then
Noise again. But everything is muffled and strange.

Where am I.

Am
I
Dead?
Everything
Is
Dark.

Except

Oh

I'm not.
I'm not dead because I'm thinking this thought, I'm
feeling this ah
This pain

I'm telling my lungs to

(*Sucking in air.*) Huuuuuuuh

Breathe

Where am I?
It's dark.
It's dark and wet / I can't see / my head hurts / can't
hear / what's going / what's going

I was in the hospital and then
And now I'm –

Huuuuuh

Ah!

A sliver of light

Is that
Daylight
I'm in a cave /
Why would I be in a cave /
is that a tooth?
Teeth? /
A mouth
I'm in its fucking mouth I'm on its tongue / I'm
lying on its tongue

it ate me

/ it swallowed me whole
I need to get out it stinks
In here
I need / to get out
Fresh air
I need

No w–
The ground is moving
The ground is / I'm being swallowed
Back towards the back of its mouth /
Tongue pushing me down / down its throat
Can't hold on
I'm being / swallowed
Swallowed alive and

Oh!

Hi Mom!
My mom is reading me a –
My dad is making chilli for –
I've grazed my knee and it hurts it –
We're in the airport and we're going on vacation
and I'm –

I'm opening my birthday present and it's a it's it's a
oh my god –
The taste of my high-school cafeteria
The smell of my first rock concert
The feeling in my gut on my first day as a med
student –
The music
The music at the party where I met –
Steve
Hi
Steve
I'm there
Right
Back
At
The
First
Day
Of
Being
In
Love
With
Steve
Oh
Wow
Steve
I'm
Sorry
I
Wish
I
Could
Put
My
Head
On
Your
Shoulder
Again
I

Wish
We
Could
Go
To
The
Movies
Again
I
Wish
We
Could
Go
To
The
Beach
And
Drink
Beer
Again
I
Wish
We
Could
Fight
Again
I
Wish
We
Could
Meet
Again
I
Wish
I
Could
Make
You
Laugh
Again
Oh

God
It
Was
All
Wonderful
Wasn't
It

Was all
So
Wonderful!

I wish I could see more of it
I wish I could see it all our wonderful terrible
wonderful terrible wonderful terrible future

I
Am
So
Happy
To
Have
Been

Alive –

A rumbling from the deep.

I'm nearly at the stomach.

I can't move my arms
I can feel the walls of the oesophagus forcing me
down
Squeezing me so tight
Can't breathe
Can't

Blacking
Out –

Black

Black

Black

Bl

Everything stops.

Everything starts again.

23. A different hospital

Sounds of a hospital.

Oh

I am in a hospital

bed.

Everything hurts.

And in the chair next to me

In the chair next to me is Steve.

Hi Steve.

Hi.

He tells me that I was eaten alive.

Yeah. I say. I'm aware.

He tells me that as far as they know, I am the only
person out of thousands that survived being eaten
which must mean

That I tasted awful.

And then he says sorry, he's so sorry, whatever our
future holds for us, he doesn't care. He wants to
spend it together.

Okay.

And then he asks me what's the last thing
I remember?

I

I came to in a park with a woman standing over me
saying help was on the way.

She said help was on the way and then she said the
strangest thing

She told me she was so sorry the ULSA had hurt me.

She was sorry that the ULSA had hurt me because she was its

mother.

The Mother Again

Sounds of Taylor.

MOM   I knew it was Taylor right away.

From the moment he came out of the ocean in Tokyo.
What kind of a parent would I be if I didn't recognise my own son?
I knew that it was Taylor, I knew that he was going to hurt a lot of people and I knew that I had to stop him.

I mean he'd changed. Changed a lot. He didn't really look like himself any more, his beautiful hair was all gone, his skin had changed to that sort of lizardy texture –

And, obviously, he was three hundred feet tall.
I held him in my arms and now he was as big as a skyscraper. It's hard to get your head around that.
I couldn't imagine the things that must have happened to him in the time we'd been apart, the change that he'd been through –

But if I looked closely

If I really looked – The way he walked. The way he sounded. And of course the eyes. It was him.

Sounds of Taylor.

I watched all morning, glued to the TV.
I was watching live when he came out of the water.
I was watching live when he headed inland and
I was watching live when he started destroying the city.
All the joy and relief that I had felt knowing that he was still alive was suddenly replaced by heartbreak.
Heartbreak for my son who was lost and alone. But

also heartbreak for the people he was hurting.
I knew right then that I had to do something. That it
was up to his parents to stop him. Because if we
didn't, who else would?

Sounds of Taylor.

That's when I texted his father to say that our son
was still alive.

He called me right back. It was the first time that
we'd spoken in years. His voice was shaky.
I asked him. Do you see it? And he said that he
didn't know what I was talking about.
I said, that thing on TV, in Japan. The ULSA. That's
Taylor! You must be able to see it!
Of course he told me it was all in my head. He told
me I was imagining things.
But I could tell from his voice. He knew. He knew
that the ULSA was his son and he was scared.

Sounds of Taylor.

I decided I would have to handle it without him.
I was desperate to go to Japan to see Taylor.
I knew that if I could just get face to face with him.
See him again, I could calm him down. Make it all
better.
But there were no flights in or out. So all I could do
was watch as the death toll went up and up.

Of course, I tried to make myself feel better.
I told myself that all this death and destruction, it
wasn't only on me.
I wasn't the one who gave up on him, after all.
I wasn't the one abandoned him in the woods, who
fucking let him go out into the world all alone. If
we had kept things going my way, if we had kept
him contained, at home then a lot less people would
have died but

But
I was his still his mom. He was in this world,
because of me. I had seen the warning signs,

first-hand, and I hadn't done anything about them
And now –

Sounds of Taylor.

When he left Japan in ruins and disappeared back
into the ocean, the whole world thought that was the
end of it. Nobody expected another ULSA attack.
But I did. I knew Taylor, I knew that he would get
hungry again, because he always did and when that
happened –
But I still believed, if I could see him again.
When he appeared in Hawaii and headed to the
West Coast. I knew I would get my chance. He was
coming home.

Sounds of Taylor.

I waited for him on my favourite part of the
Alameda shoreline
Right in the shadow of the Bay Bridge
There were people all along the coast.
People drinking, people filming, people praying

And then

We saw a surge
A shadow in the deep and from where I was stood
I could just make out
A spiny tail
Snaking through the water
Before
My son
Right in front of me, rose up, to his full magnificent
height.

Sounds of Taylor.

Watching him standing against the San Francisco
skyline, illuminated by gunfire, I thought that my
heart would burst.

He roared and then he waded out of the water and
into San Francisco, taking out the bridge as he
went.

Sounds of Taylor.
Sounds of Taylor.
Sounds of Taylor.

I knew that I needed to follow him, get as close to
him as I could.
I stole one of those tourist motorboats and I made
my way across the bay. The water was terrifying
churning and churning. It was filled with people and
cars and bodies –

Somehow I made it across. San Francisco was like a
war zone.
I knew that I needed to get somewhere high where
he could see me, where I could talk to him properly,
so I headed to the Transamerica Pyramid.
There were soldiers everywhere, firing at the sky.
People running, people crying, people screaming.
Tanks and planes and missiles and
I wanted to tell them. It's not his fault. It's not his
fault! Don't hurt him!

Sounds of Taylor.

When I got to the Transamerica the elevators
weren't working.
I took the stairs.

By the time I reached the forty-eighth floor

The rain was torrential and the tower was swaying.

One of the sides of the building had been torn away,
and the whole floor was exposed to the wind

And there, in the distance, I could see my son.

Taylor was in the south of the city, tearing the roof
from Zuckerberg General Hospital. I watched as he
turned around and started to walk in my direction.
This was it.

I was going to see him again! My baby!

As he drew closer

I tried to get his attention
I yelled 'Taylor, Taylor, it's mom I'm here!'

But the wind and the rain and the gunfire.

I kept going
'Taylor, Taylor, please! Taylor please!'
And then suddenly he turned around. He stopped
fighting and smashing and eating and turned his
gigantic head around and he faced me.

And I swear
I swear to this day that he was smiling.

Sounds of Taylor.

It was an amazing moment.
I could feel his breath.
I could smell his smell.

I reached out my hand and touched the edge of his
nose, and I knew that it was now or never.
And so I said
'Hi Taylor, hi baby boy. It's me. You know me,
don't you? It's Mom.'

Sounds of Taylor.

'Yeah.
It is so good to see you. I've missed you so much.
God I have.'

Sounds of Taylor.

'I know. I know. I know you're angry, and scared.
And I'm sorry, I'm so sorry that we let you down
that we didn't keep you safe but
You need to stop all this. You need to stop because
it's too much, honey, people are getting hurt a lot of
people and I know you don't want that.

(*Sings.*) 'Hush little baby, don't say a word,
Mama's gonna buy you a mocking-bird.
And if that mocking-bird don't sing
Mama's gonna buy you a diamond ring...'

Sounds of Taylor.

'Shhhh. Shhh. It's okay. Shhhh.'

Taylor was calm. Everything had stopped. We were together again.

Sounds of Taylor.

We were so peaceful.

I could have stayed in that moment forever.

But of course, just like that. The peace was shattered.

An army helicopter appeared out of nowhere and opened fire and suddenly, Taylor was angry again. He lifted up his head, swatted the helicopter away and then vomited onto the ground below.

Without looking back at me, he stomped away
through the city, smashing and roaring
And that was that.
The last time that I ever saw him.

Sounds of Taylor.

I'd failed.
I failed to calm him down. Failed to stop him hurting people. Failed to bring him home. And now the whole world was going to pay for it.

At the bottom of the Transam tower
I found a young doctor
Still in their scrubs
Who was lying
Half-dead on the grass.

She had been swallowed by Taylor
And then vomited up. Somehow, she was alive.
A miracle.

I like to think
He knew what he was doing.
That sparing the doctor's life
Was his small way
Of listening to me.

But I don't know.

I sat down beside her and waited for help to come.
In the distance
I watched my son's silhouette
Get smaller
Against the fiery skyline.

And under my breath
I let myself say
Goodbye.

The Future

1.

DAD   The creature that first appeared in Tokyo
Is not my son.

Nor did my son
Ever eat people.

I can't believe I have to say that.

Taylor, almost certainly, died somewhere in
Montgomery Woods.
And my losing him
Was a horrible accident. One that I will live with
forever. There is no more mystery to it than that.

I don't hate his mother for it. In a way, I'm jealous
that she doesn't have to live in the reality that I do.

I wish, just as much as she does, I could see my son
again.

I wish I could tell him that

I love him

And that

That

I'm sorry I let him down.

More than anything, I wish, just like his mom,
I wish that I could find out what happened to him.
Find out the truth.

But I can't

So that's that.

We're both doomed

Tortured in our own different ways

By the agony

Of

Never knowing.

2.

MOM   In the time since San Francisco was destroyed, my
son Taylor has reappeared in twenty-seven different
cities. Millions have died.
I still wake up every day thinking about how lonely
he must be. How scared.
Sometimes, to make myself feel better
I imagine him in those moments where he's
swimming
At the bottom of the ocean.
I think about all the wonderful things he must be
seeing. The experiences he must be having.
Things I could never have dreamt for him.
All anyone talks about is how to destroy him. But if
you ask me, the moment's passed. They won't be
able to stop him now.
I know my son. I know that he will keep eating and
eating and eating until there's nothing left to eat.
We had our chance, and we blew it.
Of course his father still won't acknowledge that
Taylor is the ULSA. He won't acknowledge that the
little boy we raised, the little boy that he abandoned
grew up to destroy cities and tear down skyscrapers.

And, you know, who can blame him?

After all

Who wants to be responsible

for the end of the world?

Sounds of Taylor.

End.

www.nickhernbooks.co.uk

facebook.com/nickhernbooks

twitter.com/nickhernbooks